NORTHERN IRELAND 1921-1971

NORTHERN IRELAND 1921-1971

by HUGH SHEARMAN

Printed by W. & G. Baird Limited, Belfast
for Her Majesty's Stationery Office

CONTENTS

	Pages
Foreword	vii
1. In the Beginning	9
2. The 'Home Rule' Question	12
3. The First Parliament	16
4. Problems of Government	19
5. Struggle for Survival	22
6. The 1925 Agreement	26
7. Divisions and Recession	29
PICTORIAL SECTION	
8. Administration—Reducing the Leeway	169
9. Jurisdiction—Eire Claim Repudiated	173
10. War and Peace	176
11. Welfare State: Industrial Development	180
12. Years of Achievement	185

This short history was commissioned by the Government of Northern Ireland to mark the 50th anniversary of the State. The author was given complete freedom to express his views.

Foreword

The year 1971 sees the completion of fifty years since Northern Ireland was established as a distinct political entity under the Government of Ireland Act of 1920; and to mark the occasion the Government of Northern Ireland decided to sponsor the publication of an illustrated book giving a brief sketch of events and developments during that half century. In inviting me to write the text of this book, the Government left me a completely free hand.

In trying to decide what such a book might most usefully contain, one felt at once that it ought not to be a mere coffee-table picture book or a poker-faced eulogy or a rollcall of provincial personalities, nor should it offer the kind of statistical information which can readily be found elsewhere. The course chosen has been to tell the story in terms of the political, social and economic forces which have given the people of the province both their great successes and their direst conflicts and problems.

This has imposed a difficult task of selection whose manner of accomplishment will perhaps please nobody. It has been made more difficult by a relative absence of serious research by others into primary sources for most of the themes of recent Northern Ireland history, by the brevity imposed by the plan of this book, and, above all, by the violent controversies which have surrounded nearly every topic which has to be referred to. The text of this book may therefore best be read as simply an interim report from one person who has lived in Northern Ireland through these fifty years, a fascinated observer of all that half century of events here described. The interim nature of what is said must be particularly evident with respect to the disturbed period at the close of the half century that is reviewed. A passage of some years would be necessary before such things can be described and discussed as historical events.

As for the sources of information used, there was plenty of material for the period just prior to the setting up of the Government of Northern Ireland. There were many political biographies and some general studies, including in particular *The Ulster Crisis* by Mr. A. T. Q. Stewart. But these sources almost completely dry up as one approaches the fifty years of Northern Ireland's actual political existence. *Craigavon, Ulsterman* by Mr. St. John Ervine is virtually the only closely relevant political biography, and *Northern Ireland in the Second World War* by Professor J. W. Blake the only detailed and scholarly narrative of events. On the legal and constitutional side we have the early work on *The Constitution of Northern Ireland* by Sir A. S. Quekett, and a valuable modern study of *Constitutional Law in Northern Ireland* by Professor Harry Calvert. A large and more or less ephemeral critical and controversial literature does, of course, record events and judgments, but generally with too little or too much detachment from actual events. I depended largely, therefore, on the contemporary press, on the reports of commissions of enquiry or other similar bodies, and on the statistical and other material produced down the years by public departments. As a guide to these last two sources and a summary of much that they contain, the volumes of *The Ulster Year Book* are so lucid and useful that one wishes that other governments would imitate its style and methods of presenting information to the public.

Finally, one wonders if there is a moral to it all? A friend to whom I once gave a volume of Irish history told me that it depressed him deeply because it made him realise that if he had been any of the actors in the story, with their particular limitations of character, circumstances and belief, he would have done exactly what they did. Such a realisation should prompt us to compassion and sympathy even towards those whose acts we most deplore and whose attitudes are most alien to us. But I believe that we can go further than this. In recognising these determinisms which have moulded the lives of others, we can ourselves become to some extent free of them and so able to choose more freely for ourselves what kind of Ulster we want.

1. In the Beginning

'There have come to be two interacting cultures, separated by differences in religion, education and loyalties, keeping apart in spite of some intermarriage and much intermingling in business. Yet they have shared many experiences and have been much thrown together, and together they have given the Province its own distinctive regional character, different from that of the Irish Republic or from any region of Great Britain.'

While the purpose of this book is to tell the story of Northern Ireland during fifty years of its political and constitutional existence as a partly self-governing province of the United Kingdom under the Government of Ireland Act 1920, it is necessary also to describe some of the events which occurred before 1920. That Northern Ireland has had a distinctive separate political history of its own in the present century is the natural outcome of the fact that it had, during many preceding centuries, a history which was often somewhat separate from that of the rest of Ireland and the rest of the British Isles.

Certain geographical factors which are only of minor importance today had in past centuries a powerful influence upon communities before modern transport, land usage, engineering and drainage had taken effect. In particular, the lakes and rivers, swamps and forests of south Ulster were at one time a formidable strategic barrier, segregating Ulster from the rest of Ireland to an extent that is today hard to imagine.

Proximity to Scotland also gave Ulster a special role in the prehistory of Ireland, causing it to become a bridgehead by which migrating peoples entered the island. Ulster was the first part of Ireland to become populated after the end of the last ice age; and primitive stone implements found on the north shore of Lough Neagh are about 8,000 years old.

It is characteristic of the part which geographical factors played in Northern Ireland's prehistory that, about 2,500 BC, the province provided the location of a distinctive megalithic culture, whose great stone monuments are slightly different from those found in other parts of Ireland. It is sometimes called the cult of the horned cairn, and its monuments are distributed over a territory almost identical with that of the modern Northern Ireland.

About the beginning of the Christian era Ulster emerged from prehistory into the obscure morning twilight of history as a kingdom whose mythical hero Cuchulainn, and the knights of the Red Branch, were engaged in long and violent wars with the warriors of the other kingdoms of Ireland.

The name Ulster is often used as a second name for Northern Ireland. The name was once Uladh, and the 'ster' ending was added much later by Scandinavian invaders who similarly added it to Leinster and Munster. The area to which the name Ulster was applied has varied a good deal. The Ulster kingdom which was ruled by Conor macNessa and championed by Cuchulainn was much larger than the modern Northern Ireland and stretched to the Boyne and the Shannon. A later kingdom of Ulster consisted of little more than the modern counties of Down and Antrim. Ulster as a province consisting of nine counties, of which three are in the Irish Republic and six in Northern Ireland, was simply a definition of convenience imposed for administrative purposes by English officials at the close of the sixteenth century and is not rooted in the ancient Irish past. Thus County Cavan was quite arbitrarily transferred from Connaught to Ulster in the early seventeenth century.

Through the long intervening centuries between the ancient Ulster and the modern Ulster, whose history may be said to have begun early in the seventeenth century, the essential element of continuity lay in the fact that the heart of Ulster remained intact and was not penetrated by that piecemeal English conquest which affected nearly every other part of Ireland. Behind its natural geographical defences, the northern province was never wholly penetrated or overrun by outside invaders until the very end of the sixteenth century. Dominated by the great families of O'Neill and O'Donnell, it remained a last fortress of native resistance, a last stronghold of ancient Gaelic language, social custom, culture and tradition. It was also the heartland of those ancient pagan stories of the loves and battles and death of Cuchulainn, the sorrows of Deirdre, and many more which caught the imagination of later generations. And, since it contained the scenes of St. Patrick's first labours in Ireland, and his archiepiscopal see at Armagh, it was also the historic heart of Christian Ireland.

One can feel much sympathy for those who represent an ancient and heroic tradition. One can also understand why, under dangerous pressure from Spain and other continental enemies, the government of Elizabeth I felt that it was urgently necessary in their time to bring the aristocratic independence of the O'Neills and O'Donnells to an end and to bring the whole province of Ulster under English law and control. After nine years of strenuous warfare the end came as the old queen lay dying. James I began his reign in 1603 with the opportunity to make a new settlement of Irish affairs, particularly in Ulster.

After several years of effort to reach an improbable compromise with O'Neill and O'Donnell, who at last withdrew to the continent, it was decided that the best course was to introduce British colonists into Ulster. It was a territory with large resources and a sparse population. Ideas of colonisation were in the air at the time, particularly with respect to America.

Francis Bacon, the Solicitor General, particularly advised James I that the scheme for the 'plantation' of Ulster should aim not just at introducing English landowners who would have native Irish tenants and workers but at establishing a complete British and Protestant community of all classes, tenants and workers as well as landed proprietors. This policy was adopted. Landed estates were offered on easy terms to English and Scottish 'undertakers' who were to introduce tenants who were British and Protestant.

In 1610 immigration into Ulster from England and Scotland began and proceeded apace under the supervision of Plantation Commissioners. The counties of Antrim and Down did not form part of the special plantation area, but into these also there came a very substantial British immigrant population. These two eastern counties had the advantage of easy access across the narrow sea to England and Scotland. With the encouragement of Sir Arthur Chichester, the head of the administration in Ireland, many Devon men settled in the little town of Belfast. A few other immigrants there came from the Isle of Man.

To the nucleus thus established there came later a steady stream of newcomers, mostly from Scotland to avoid the persecuting rule of Lauderdale in the time of Charles II, but also some from France to avoid the persecution of Protestants by Louis XIV, some from Germany with the armies of the early Hanoverian kings, and some through ordinary private motives of trading, self-betterment or perhaps escape from justice.

There was obviously quite a lot of intermingling of the various immigrants with the native Irish population. In the course of three hundred years the population that has come to inhabit Ulster represents a blend of people that is unique. Inevitably it has developed a strong regional flavour, with its own dialects and ways of speech which carry some record of the strong Scottish ingredient in the population and of the Shakespearian days in which the Plantation was first established.

There remains to this day, also, a pattern of duality which still reflects the division of newcomers and natives, Protestants and Roman Catholics. There have come to be two interacting cultures, separated by differences in religion, education and loyalties, keeping apart in spite of some intermarriage and much intermingling in business. Yet they have shared many experiences and have been much thrown together, and together they have given the province its own distinctive regional character, different from that of the Irish Republic or from any region of Great Britain.

Isolation and danger in the seventeenth century also served to give the new immigrant Ulster community a strong political and social self-consciousness. During the 1640's and 50's English Royalists, Parliamentarians, Scots and insurgent Irish all battled for control of the province. Later in the century the armies of James II occupied parts of Ulster and failed after a long siege to capture Londonderry. In 1690 the forces of William of Orange brought security and victory for the British and Protestant cause by winning the battle of the Boyne. This event, desperately crucial for the survival of the Protestant community in Ulster, is annually celebrated in the province to this day.

Thus, although Northern Ireland's formal separate political existence dates only from 1921, it could fairly be said that Northern Ireland existed socially and even politically for three hundred years before that.

In certain fields the political influence of the Ulster Protestant community came to be strongly radical and liberal. There was a strong sympathy with the American and French revolutions. In the eighteenth century many moved on from Ulster to the American colonies to form what American historians have often called the 'Scotch Irish'. They formed a high proportion of the population of the colonies at the time of the Declaration of American Independence and provided a large part of the leadership and the rank and file of the American forces in the War of Independence. An Ulster link with the United States of America has endured ever since.

At home the radical sympathies of Ulster Protestants emerged in a fierce rejection of the project of making Belfast a slave-trading port like Liverpool or Bristol. They emerged in agitation against excessive restriction of Irish trade and of the Dublin parliament. They emerged when representatives of 143 corps of volunteers, all Protestants, met in the town of Dungannon in 1782 and among other resolutions passed, with only two dissentients, the following:—'Resolved, That we hold the right of private judgment in matters of religion to be equally sacred in others as in ourselves. Resolved, therefore, That as men and as Irishmen, as Christians and Protestants, we rejoice in the relaxation of the penal laws against our Roman Catholic fellow subjects, and that we conceive the measure to be fraught with the happiest consequences to the union and prosperity of the inhabitants of Ireland.'

On the other hand, wherever people felt themselves threatened and their economic and social security in danger, there was also in Ulster a strong reactionary tendency. Traditional fears of the native Irish which had haunted the first settlers in the seventeenth century had been directed not so much against the common people as against their aristocratic leaders; and the penal laws had been devised at the behest of the great Anglo-Irish landowners, who dominated the Dublin parliament, for the purpose of bringing about a social down-grading of the Roman Catholic and originally Gaelic-speaking aristocracy.

This purpose was largely successful, and for the most part, the Roman Catholic element in the population of Ulster in the eighteenth century had no alternative but to be passive and inert, while all the social and political decision-making went on over their heads among Protestant landlords and masters.

When the penal laws were relaxed, however—as so many Ulster Protestants thought it right they should be—it became possible for Roman Catholics to emerge as competitors with their Protestant neighbours for leases of land. Already the downtrodden Roman Catholic Irish had been used by landlords to undercut Protestant tenants of land who were less prepared to pay exorbitant rents or accept harshly exacting terms. Indeed this undercutting had been one of the causes of Ulster Protestant emigration to America. Threatened in their livelihood and where they were most vulnerable, substantial numbers of Protestant small farmers in Ulster, as elsewhere in Ireland, reacted bitterly and aggressively. Many parts of Ireland in the middle and later years of the eighteenth century were disturbed by outrages committed by rival terrorist gangs, as differences which had previously been religious were more sharply felt as economic. In Ulster, Protestant 'Peep o' Day Boys' raided and wrecked the homes and property of Roman Catholic farmers and Roman Catholic 'Defenders' retaliated. And these tensions grew as the population of the countryside steadily increased towards a desperate condition of over-population.

These two themes, therefore, have run through the dominant Protestant element in the life of Ulster, with echoes going down to the present day. There is a strong liberal, progressive and humanitarian tradition, and also a self-defensively reactionary tradition which is activated when there is anxiety and pressure.

And always living among and alongside the Ulster Protestants were the Roman Catholics. They had been deprived during the eighteenth century of all leadership except that of their own clergy who had stood by them with a stubborn heroism that is remembered with gratitude to this day. As conditions of life very slowly improved for the Roman Catholics they became increasingly self-conscious as a social group and desired to assert and better themselves.

2. The Home Rule Question

'We pledge ourselves in solemn Covenant throughout this our time of threatened calamity to stand by one another in defending for ourselves and our children our cherished position of equal citizenship in the United Kingdom.'

Up to the end of the eighteenth century Ireland was governed by an administration in Dublin and there was an Irish parliament which was subordinate to the British government in London. The Irish parliament was not a democratic institution and was dominated and manipulated by the great Anglo-Irish Protestant landowners in alliance with the British government. In 1800, however, the Act of Union was passed in the two parliaments, at Westminster and in Dublin, and Ireland was united with Great Britain in one United Kingdom of Great Britain and Ireland.

The Union was not opposed by any substantial element in the population of Ireland, but its great defect was that it was not accompanied by legislation to give full political and legal rights of citizenship to all, regardless of religion. The expectation that this would be done indeed won much support for the project of the Union, and, at the time, only one Roman Catholic bishop in Ireland expressed himself against it. But the actual granting of equality of citizenship and of legal rights was not accomplished until 1829 and then only after much agitation.

It is important to notice that some of the remaining legal disabilities which Irish Roman Catholics had suffered were also shared by the many Ulster Protestants who were not members of the established Anglican Church. For example, the marriages of Presbyterians had not been strictly legal if they were not celebrated according to the rites of the Established Church, and Presbyterians were not eligible for certain offices. The removal of Presbyterian grievances helped to unite Protestants in Ulster, and this was still further facilitated when, in 1870, the Church of Ireland, the Protestant episcopal church, was disestablished and became an independent voluntary church.

The nineteenth century, while Ireland was part of the United Kingdom, at first saw great suffering and hardship in an over-crowded, poverty-stricken and famine-ridden land. This suffering reached its climax in the great famine of the 1840's which led to a steadily falling population and to emigration on a large scale. But the later nineteenth century was a time of progress and reform, from which Ulster gained more advantage than most other parts of Ireland.

Apart from special reforms devised for Ireland, the Union now brought the opportunity for participation in the social and economic progress of Britain. Religious liberty and equality were established. The right to vote was given to large classes of the population who had never had it before. Ulster became heavily industrialised and prospered greatly by freely selling in Britain the produce of its farms, factories and shipyards. Gradually, as in Britain, there also came the beginnings of public health administration and of local government, better housing, better education, better working conditions, the beginnings of a trade union movement. And throughout Ireland, as the result of the Irish Land Acts, there was a government-sponsored revolution in land ownership by which ownership of their farms came to nearly all farmers, who in the past had been only insecure rent-paying tenants of the land they worked.

With more favourable conditions there developed throughout a large part of Ireland an increasingly organised opposition to the Union and a growing demand for self-government. The new nineteenth century sentiment of nationalism had reached Ireland. Its emergence only served to deepen the cleavage between Protestant and Catholic in Ulster. While it gripped the Roman Catholics throughout Ireland it did not touch the Protestant majority in the north-east corner of the island, by whom the great advantages of the Union were much more appreciated.

In 1885 Mr. Gladstone, the Prime Minister at the head of a Liberal Government, declared himself in favour of partial self-government for Ireland, the policy popularly called Home Rule. This event united in vigorous opposition all who wished the Union to continue unimpaired, and the heart of this opposition to Home Rule was in Ulster.

The prospect of Home Rule was feared by a large proportion of the population in Ulster for three main reasons. First, it would place a predominantly Protestant community in Ulster under a predominantly Roman Catholic Dublin government. Secondly, it would place a predominantly British community under the rule of a government dominated by what was felt to be an unpredictable alien nationalism. Thirdly, it would place the expanding industrial life of Ulster under a government dominated by almost wholly agricultural interests.

Although the measure of Home Rule proposed by Gladstone was very limited, there was a tendency for Irish nationalists to speak of it only as a beginning and even to speculate about a day when an Irish government could exclude British goods from Ireland by tariffs. Ulster opposition to Home Rule was thus intensified by the view that the proposed legislation was only the thin end of a large wedge of separation from Britain which threatened the whole economic basis of life in Ulster.

Home Rule bills were defeated in 1886 and 1892. The passage of time and the continuing controversy made Ulster opposition to Home Rule much more highly organised and formidable. It also broke the old Ulster links with the Liberal party in Britain. Constituencies in the province had regularly been represented at Westminster by over a dozen Liberal members of parliament, of whom some were very radical in their views. Now the province swung to the Conservatives. This did not mean, however, that liberal and progressive sympathies died out, but they sought other outlets.

A period of Conservative rule suspended the Home Rule controversy, and when the Liberals came back to power in 1906 they did not at first renew their interest in Home Rule for Ireland. In the general election of 1910, however, they lost a great part of their House of Commons majority and so became dependent upon the support of the Irish nationalist members if they were to stay in office. The price of that support was a fresh Home Rule Bill.

A quarter of a century of fierce controversy had brought the Ulster Unionists to a high level of organisation. To co-ordinate resistance to Home Rule there was established an Ulster Unionist Council consisting of representatives of a wide variety of organisations with Unionist sympathies. In February, 1910, the Ulster Unionists invited Sir Edward Carson, a distinguished Dublin barrister, to be their leader. Carson was a brilliant advocate and a powerful orator. He represented Unionist Ulster to the world and to the House of Commons. But the man on the spot in Ulster was Captain James Craig, a veteran of the South African War and a future prime minister of Northern Ireland. Most of the crucial decisions of the next few years seem to have come from him.

The Irish Nationalists, led by John Redmond and representing the great majority of people in Ireland as a whole, were confidently pressing the government to move on briskly to implement the policy of self-government for Ireland. The Nationalists in Ulster formed an active part of this general political movement; yet, where they found themselves a minority among a predominantly Unionist population, they could not but feel that their circumstances were very different from those of their southern colleagues and their prospects less clear and encouraging.

In 1911 the Unionist leaders announced their policy. If Home Rule were imposed upon Ireland, they would establish a separate provincial government of Ulster. The Ulster Unionist Council established a commission to draft a constitution 'for the Provisional Government of Ulster, having due regard to the interests of the loyalists in other parts of Ireland, the powers and duration of such Provisional Government to come into operation on the day of the passing of any Home Rule Bill, to remain in force until Ulster shall again resume unimpaired her citizenship of the United Kingdom'. The purpose of this plan was to give the Unionists a chance to control their own destiny, to provide a basis from which they could negotiate and to prevent an outbreak of violence which was to be expected if the province were placed under a Dublin government against the will of the majority of its inhabitants.

This provisional government was actually constituted in 1913, ready to become active if required. As a further source of strength and guarantee of order in the province there was established the Ulster Volunteer Force, which grew in a couple of years to consist of 110,000 men, of whom a large proportion were armed. A retired Lieutenant-General with active fighting experience was appointed to command the force.

In September, 1912, the Ulster Covenant was signed by 471,414 Ulster people. Its text was as follows:— 'Being convinced in our conscience that Home Rule would be disastrous to the material well-being of Ulster as well as of the whole of Ireland, subversive of our civil and religious freedom, destructive of our citizenship and perilous to the unity of the Empire, we, whose names are underwritten, men of Ulster, loyal subjects of His Gracious Majesty King George V, humbly relying on the God whom our fathers in days of stress and trial confidently trusted, do hereby pledge ourselves in solemn Covenant throughout this our time of threatened calamity to stand by one another in defending for ourselves and our children our cherished position of equal citizenship in the United Kingdom and in using all means which may be found necessary to defeat the present conspiracy to set up a Home Rule Parliament in Ireland.

'And in the event of such a Parliament being forced upon us we further solemnly and mutually pledge ourselves to refuse to recognise its authority.
'In sure confidence that God will defend the right we hereto subscribe our names.

'And further we individually declare that we have not already signed this Covenant.'

The British government was uncertain in its attitude towards these developments in Ulster. It was impossible to ignore the fact that the majority in Ireland, including a very substantial minority in Ulster itself, desired Home Rule and supported the bill that was going through parliament. In the spring of 1914, therefore, the government decided to make a show of force.

Yet even while deciding on this policy, the government was inhibited and rather demoralised by the knowledge that a very large part of the British public warmly sympathised with the Ulster Unionists and would not tolerate any idea of coercing them. The chosen time was the weekend of 21 March 1914. Plans were made for a convergence of armed forces on Ulster. The third battle squadron of the Royal Navy was ordered to proceed north. Two cruisers entered Belfast Lough and landed troops at Carrickfergus and Bangor. The orders given to the troops at the Curragh in Kildare were unclear and gave the impression that officers not desiring to take part in military action against the Ulster Unionists might resign their commissions. In the outcome the whole operation was brought to a standstill by the high proportion of officers who made it clear that they would not participate in it. The project was abandoned and the Secretary of State for War had to resign.

Meanwhile plans to bring in a cargo of arms to the Ulster Unionists proceeded quietly. On the night of 24 April 1914, occurred the Ulster gun-running, a well organised and successful operation.

Already the notion had been discussed of temporarily excluding Ulster or part of Ulster from the operation of the Home Rule Bill. All that had happened during the preceding years had asserted the existence of 'Ulster' as a formidable political entity. Carson took the realistic view that, for practical purposes, 'Ulster' at that time was the area of six counties now forming Northern Ireland, and this was the area whose exclusion was discussed.

But, if the government was under pressure from Ulster Unionists, it was also under powerful pressure from Irish nationalists demanding Home Rule. The formation of the Ulster Volunteers had done much to encourage the formation of another and larger body, the Irish National Volunteers who supported the national cause.

The summer of 1914 saw nothing settled. The Home Rule legislation though not yet in operation, had become law. The Ulster Unionist leaders expected at any moment to put their provisional government plans into action and carry out the *coup d'état* that would put them in collision alike with the British government and with the Irish nationalists.

Seeing powerful political interests set on what seemed a course of unavoidable violent collision, the political leaders caught in a disastrous deadlock, and an irresolute government, with a weak parliamentary position, staggering on the edge of civil war in Ireland, King George V intervened personally and called a conference at Buckingham Palace on 21 July. At this conference Carson and Craig participated as principals, representing the Ulster Unionists. The conference failed.

On 26 July the National Volunteers had their gun-running at Howth, Co. Dublin. This led to a collison with the army in which three persons were killed and thirty-eight wounded.

At the beginning of August came the outbreak of the First World War and the perilous situation in Ireland was transformed. The Ulster Volunteer Force was placed unreservedly at Britain's service, and at first many nationalists and members of the National Volunteers equally threw themselves into the war effort.

The war and the conditions which it created did much to clarify the situation in Ireland. It showed that the Ulster Unionists were ready to accept every sacrifice which the Union demanded of them as well as claim its advantages. They served with great heroism in the armed services in nearly every battle of the war and suffered very heavy casualties, particularly in 1916 when the 36th (Ulster) Division lost 5,500 officers and men in two days at Thiepval in the battle of the Somme. But a more tragic sacrifice was demanded of those quite numerous nationalists who also served with heroism and suffered heavy casualties in the British forces and yet were afterwards largely disowned by the new revolutionary Ireland which came into being during the war.

That same year, 1916, had seen the Easter week republican rising in Dublin. This, and the reactions which followed upon it, transformed the whole character of Irish political nationalism in less than three years, putting political control into the hands of those who had decided to have an independent republic created by their own actions and not a settlement based on any vote or negotiations in London.

The general election of 1918 showed up the new position. From Ulster twenty-six Unionist members were sent to Westminster. Through the rest of Ireland the new republican Sinn Fein party won seventy-three seats, while the old Irish Nationalist party was reduced to only six. The victorious Sinn Fein candidates did not go to Westminster but met in Dublin as Dail Eireann and published a declaration of independence.

A complete parting of the ways had come. It only remained to see in what constitutional form—if any—these vast differences of loyalty and sympathy, and perhaps above all of temperament, could be peacefully expressed and contained.

3. The First Parliament

'. . . I appeal to all Irishmen to pause, to stretch out the hand of forbearance and conciliation, to forgive and forget, and to join in making for the land which they love a new era of peace, contentment and goodwill.'

The state of civil war which had seemed imminent in Ireland in 1914 became a reality after 1918. The conflict was not primarily between north and south. It was between two completely conflicting views of legality and of what constituted lawful government. The United Kingdom government continued to attempt to carry on the administration of Ireland, but throughout a great part of the island its authority was challenged by the rival claim of an Irish Republic, constituted in a revolutionary fashion, which treated Britain as an enemy and endeavoured to enforce its own claims to govern. In this way the greater part of Ireland was reduced to a state of guerrilla warfare and anarchy, in which the Unionist areas of the north were only less gravely disturbed than other parts.

The British government now attempted to provide a new political settlement for Ireland, based on the establishment of two subordinate parliaments, one for the north and one for the south; and it is from this that the modern constitution of Northern Ireland came into being.

The aim of the British government was to devise a settlement which would retain all Ireland within the United Kingdom, give reasonable recognition and scope to the communal differences in Ireland and yet provide a means for their ultimate reconciliation if both sides desired it.

The Government of Ireland Act of 1920 was really a fourth Home Rule Bill; but it differed from the three earlier Home Rule Bills by leaving a great part of Ulster in separate control of its own affairs. It was a compromise. The north was to accept Home Rule and the south was to accept and tolerate the social and other characteristics which differentiated the north from the rest of Ireland and allow it to choose its own way of life in a good many respects. And no door was shut against future friendship, co-operation or even unity as between north and south.

It was frankly a Home Rule measure, and as such it demanded of the Ulster Unionists a climb-down and a concession which ran contrary to old principles; but at the same time it removed the sources of several of the most emphatic northern objections to Home Rule by not placing Ulster Unionists under a Dublin government or under majority Roman Catholic rule and by giving them a limited government of their own which, in their hands, could always be a strong bargaining advantage in any further controversy or negotiations.

In the outcome the Unionists agreed to accept this settlement. A circumstance which must strongly have influenced them in its favour was that they themselves had been thinking along those lines ever since 1911 when they had projected their own scheme for a provisional government of Ulster. Indeed that earlier project had been a valuable educational experience for those who were going to be leaders and members of a future government of Northern Ireland. It had forced them to think realistically for several years about what the establishment of such a government would entail and what would have to be done by those who administered it. In addition many of them had had practical experience either in parliament or in local government or in some form of public administration or in legal work or in the armed services; and this also gave them a realistic appreciation of what had to be done and how it could be done and disposed them to accept an actual situation rather than take entrenched positions behind theoretical doctrinaire principles or make impossible demands. Experience, in fact, gave them a certain moderation in their outlook and enabled them to get what they wanted because they restrained themselves from wanting more than they could have.

In accepting a provincial parliament for Northern Ireland, the Ulster Unionists agreed that the area within which this parliament was to function should be six counties and not the nine-county Ulster which had been created by the government of James I. The reason for this was simply that, if the larger area had been included under the rule of the new government of Northern Ireland, the Unionists might not have felt entirely confident of retaining control over it.

The position was candidly explained by Craig in the House of Commons at Westminster on 29 March 1920, in the following words:

'If we had a nine-counties parliament, with 64 members, the Unionist majority would be about 3 or 4, but in a six-counties parliament, with 52 members, the Unionist majority would be about 10. The three excluded counties contain some 70,000 Unionists and 260,000 Sinn Feiners and Nationalists, and the addition of that large stock of Sinn Feiners and Nationalists, would reduce our majority to such a level that no sane man would undertake to carry on a parliament with it . . . Nothing was more heartrending to us than to take the decision which we felt we had to take a few days ago in Belfast when we decided more or less that our Unionist fellow countrymen in the 3 counties of Monaghan, Cavan and Donegal should remain outside the Ulster parliament.'

The form which the Act of 1920 took, therefore, was to define the area of Northern Ireland and then state that the rest of Ireland was 'Southern Ireland'. 'For the purpose of this Act, Northern Ireland shall consist of the parliamentary counties of Antrim, Armagh, Down, Fermanagh, Londonderry and Tyrone, and the parliamentary boroughs of Belfast and Londonderry, and Southern Ireland shall consist of so much of Ireland as is not comprised within the said parliamentary counties and boroughs.'

In each case, whether north or south, the new regional parliament was to consist of the King, a senate and a house of commons. Today the Act of 1920 has to be read as applying to Northern Ireland only; but at the time of its passing it was intended, not only that the Act should set up two parliaments but, very optimistically, that it should provide a means by which, with their own simultaneous common consent, these might later be replaced by a single all-Ireland parliament. The machinery by which this outcome was to be encouraged was a Council of Ireland on which 13 members from each house of commons and 7 senators from each parliament should sit with a president appointed by the Crown to deal with matters of common interest—'the promotion of mutual intercourse and uniformity in relation to matters affecting the whole of Ireland' and 'providing for the administration of services which the two parliaments mutually agree should be administered uniformly throughout the whole of Ireland'. And if the two parliaments agreed and passed identical acts of their own to that effect, the Act permitted them to establish a single parliament which would take over the work of both the two regional parliaments and of the Council of Ireland.

Under the Act a general election was held to elect members to the two parliaments. The method of election was a form of proportional representation. In Southern Ireland Sinn Fein had an unopposed victory in 124 seats out of 128, even though in the 1918 general election Sinn Fein had not secured a majority of the available votes in Ireland as a whole and might have had considerably less success if it had accepted normal democratic processes and not used strong-arm methods. The four southern candidates who were not Sinn Fein were non-party representatives of Dublin University, pledged only to do what they could for the protection and welfare of the university and for a peaceful settlement of Irish conflicts. In Northern Ireland, out of 52 seats, the Unionists won 40, the Nationalists 6 and Sinn Fein 6.

The first Parliament of Northern Ireland met in the City Hall in Belfast on 7 June 1921. The Lord Lieutenant of Ireland, Viscount Fitzalan, swore in the Prime Minister and Cabinet; and a Speaker, the Honourable Hugh O'Neill, was elected, and the members took the oath of allegiance. The Nationalists and the Sinn Fein members did not attend.

The first cabinet of the new Northern Ireland government consisted of the following six men:—Prime Minister, the Rt. Hon. Sir James Craig, Bt., D.L.; Minister of Finance, the Rt. Hon. Hugh MacDowell Pollock, D.L.; Minister of Home Affairs, the Rt. Hon. Richard Dawson Bates, O.B.E.; Minister of Education, the Rt. Hon. the Marquess of Londonderry, K.G., M.V.O., H.M.L.; Minister of Labour, the Rt. Hon. John Miller Andrews, D.L.; Minister of Agriculture and Minister of Commerce, the Rt. Hon. Edward Mervyn Archdale, D.L. Later John Milne Barbour, D.L., became Minister of Commerce. Thus over many years the Northern Ireland cabinet was a committee of seven people.

Twenty-four senators were to be elected by the House of Commons on the principle of proportional representation, together with the Lord Mayor of Belfast and the Mayor of Londonderry as ex-officio members. On this principle there ought to have been 18 Unionists, 3 Nationalists and 3 Sinn Fein senators; but, as the Nationalist and Sinn Fein members of the House of Commons abstained from attending and made no nominations of candidates for the senate, the senate was at first entirely Unionist.

On 22 June 1921, King George V and Queen Mary came to Belfast for the state opening of the first session of the new parliament of Northern Ireland. The presence of both the King and Queen in Belfast, at a time of riots, bomb outrages and murders, aroused both deeply affectionate gratitude and much anxiety. The royal party received an immensely cordial welcome and returned home in safety; but a train carrying men and horses of the 10th Hussars who had formed part of the King's escort was blown up, three soldiers and a guard being killed and many horses killed and mutilated.

The King's speech at the opening of parliament departed from that formality of utterance usual on such occasions and reflected a very keen personal concern. In the course of it he said: 'I speak from a full heart when I pray that my coming to Ireland today may prove to be the first step towards an end of strife among her people, whatever their race or creed. In that hope I appeal to all Irishmen to pause, to stretch out the hand of forbearance and conciliation, to forgive and forget, and to join in making for the land which they love a new era of peace, contentment and good will.' And he closed his speech by saying, "May this historic gathering be the prelude of a day in which the Irish people, north and south, under one parliament or two, as these parliaments may themselves decide, shall work together in common love for Ireland upon the sure foundations of mutual justice and respect.'

The parliament thus established had a house of commons of 52 members and a senate of 26 members. The House of Commons, as at Westminster, has a life of not more than five years before it is dissolved and a new house elected. An elected senator serves for a term of eight years, but half the elected members of the senate are elected every four years, so that the senate approximately reflects the political complexion of the commons.

The general procedure of the Northern Ireland Parliament is similar to that at Westminster, and the Senate plays a part rather like that of the House of Lords. But there are two interesting differences of procedure which may be mentioned. Because of the small number of persons involved and the desirability of avoiding needless duplication of functions, a minister can make a statement or answer a question in either house, though he may vote only in one house.

And another procedural device, which has never had to be used, was introduced to prevent a deadlock between the two houses, a constitutional problem which was still much in the public mind since the rejection by the House of Lords of the Liberal government's budget in 1909. The rule is that if or when the two houses of the Northern Ireland parliament fail to reach agreement by the ordinary procedures of passing a bill to and fro through its various readings in each house and accepting amendments, then the two houses are to meet together in one assembly and settle their differences by vote. Up to the time of writing this has never had to be done. The duties which are carried out by the Sovereign in the constitution of the United Kingdom have, since 1922, been carried out within the limits of the constitution of Northern Ireland by the Governor of Northern Ireland. The Governor summons, prorogues or dissolves the parliament of Northern Ireland and gives the final assent to its legislation. But this office was not established in the beginning, and the functions of the Crown were at first performed by the then Lord Lieutenant of Ireland, Lord Fitzalan.

The parliament met at first in the City Hall, Belfast, but soon became the tenant of the Presbyterian Theological College, a sober building at the rear of Queen's University, Belfast. It was ten years later that the foundation stone of Northern Ireland's own Parliament House at Stormont was laid.

4. Problems of Government

'Apart from its industries, which were at that time getting into a parlous state, the province was behind and inferior to the rest of Ireland in general prosperity, in agriculture, higher education and cultural facilities, in public health and in a good many other respects.'

The extent of the powers and responsibilities delegated to the new government of Northern Ireland is roughly indicated by the departments which were set up and represented by Ministers in its first cabinet. Its responsibility for internal affairs was fairly complete; but all matters which concerned the United Kingdom as a whole remained under the direct control of Westminster and Whitehall. These reserved matters included the Crown and succession, the armed forces, foreign and imperial or Commonwealth affairs, coinage, weights and measures, external trade and communications by sea and air, the post office, telephones, cables and radio, and nearly all taxation. The financial relations between the Northern Ireland government and the United Kingdom government were described in the Act of 1920, but these were somewhat modified when the southern Irish government was found not to be functioning and was presently replaced by the constitution of the Irish Free State. They were also modified by working experience. The financial aspect of Northern Ireland's constitution will be explained later.

The new government was able to draw upon quite a substantial range of talent. It had, of course, a rather provincial aspect; but, taking into consideration the relatively small population upon which the parliament and government of Northern Ireland draws its personnel, the quality of the men and women who have emerged into public life in the service of the province is very creditable. There have always been a few individuals who would clearly have been quite capable of making a career for themselves in the government of a much larger country.

The new Prime Minister, Sir James Craig, apart from his impressive career in local leadership, had held junior office at Westminster as parliamentary secretary to the Ministry of Pensions and then financial secretary to the Admiralty. He was the only member of the new government who had ever before held office in a government; but none of his colleagues was without a good deal of experience in dealing with affairs. Two of them were to be Craig's colleagues for the rest of his life—Dawson Bates at Home Affairs, who had previously been secretary to the Ulster Unionist Council, and Andrews at the Ministry of Labour, who was later to move to the Ministry of Finance and to succeed Craig as Prime Minister. Andrews came of one of the old Ulster families which had been staunchly Liberal in its political traditions but which had broken with the Liberal party when Gladstone declared himself in favour of Home Rule.

Craig himself was a simple and conventional man with nothing that one could call an intellectual or cultural life; but he had a capacity for assessing people, including himself, with great accuracy. This made him a very cool, relaxed and successful politician. He easily recognised the personalities and factors which did not require his attention or concern and so never lost vitality through minor worries. This made space in his life for the exercise of that high level of physical and political courage with which he could make crucial decisions. Most of the major decisions of the Ulster Unionist leadership had been his. Probably the supreme test of his political nerve had been that weekend in March 1914 when he had stood firm and waited, while the Government made moves to challenge him with a naval battle squadron and 25,000 troops. As he had rightly estimated, it was the government, containing men of the calibre of Asquith, Lloyd George and Winston Churchill, which lost its nerve and climbed down and not himself.

This power of decision served a resolute dedication to certain simply conceived aims and ideals. With a normal man's capacity for self-indulgence, he yet had a considerable selflessness. Well aware of his own limitations, he had no hesitation in allowing the fullest scope to the talents and ideas of others or even letting others have the credit for insights and decisions that were really his own. He was popular with civil servants who had to work with him. Above all he had great personal charm. The portraits and photographs of him that survive give little or no idea of the great natural friendliness and good humour that he carried with him. He made many friends and kept them, and some of them were among his most persistent political opponents.

Indeed it was his tolerance and understanding of opinions and attitudes opposed to his own that made him adroit and formidable in debate. It was characteristic of him that when his great opponent, the nationalist leader John Redmond, died in 1918, it was Craig who wrote a cordial appreciation of him for a London evening newspaper.

A man with these endowments of character and capacity was admirably fitted to be the head of the new government. He was steady, knew what he was doing and wanted to do, and could be a tower of strength to any colleague. And he had a certain tranquil largeness of attitude which made it unnecessary for him to exclude even the most violent of his opponents from his understanding and acceptance.

One of the first things needed was of course a civil service. This was provided largely from the civil service of the old Irish administration, the establishment symbolised by Dublin Castle. In the troubled condition of the south of Ireland, many civil servants were happy to be transferred to Belfast, and transfers were particularly sought by civil servants who were Protestants or who were themselves northerners. To these were added many local recruits, a high proportion of them being ex-servicemen. At first many appointments were temporary, but established status was quickly given to most of this new staff, and very soon the then normal machinery of entry by examination was established for the lower grades.

The first head of the Northern Ireland civil service and permanent secretary to the Ministry of Finance was an Englishman, Sir Ernest Clark. Very meticulous, hard working and hard driving, Clark, like the Prime Minister, had great social charm and those public qualities which made him in later life for twelve years a popular governor of Tasmania. Already, while an income tax official, he had been loaned for the task of establishing an income tax administration in South Africa; and he was well qualified to shape the new administration of Northern Ireland on the traditional lines of the Whitehall civil service. He is credited with having exerted a big creative influence upon the form which the financial relations between the Northern Ireland government and the government of the United Kingdom have taken over the half century which followed.

Craig's own personal contacts in London also served to recruit talent for the new government. Several civil servants close to himself came from the Admiralty, including Charles Blackmore, who later became Secretary to the cabinet.

The work of establishing the administration began in an atmosphere of constant peril and hectic improvisation. The transfer of certain vital records and papers from Dublin to Belfast was achieved only by conspiracy among such civil servants as could be relied upon, for the influence of Sinn Fein in government and administration in Dublin was entirely inimical to what was being done in Belfast. The needed documents were secretly abstracted from offices, bundled into lorries and hurried northwards with a hope that in any highway hold-up it would be imagined that they were old scrap of no importance. In the end an adequate foundation of basic documentation and paper work was achieved.

The conditions under which the work of government had to go on were established by the fact that this was the age of the Irish political gunman. Members of the government lived under constant armed guard and many prominent civil servants carried guns in their pockets.

In spite of the terms of the Government of Ireland Act, the rapid development of political change in southern Ireland had almost at once put the territorial integrity of Northern Ireland in question. The frontier, though it had been clearly indicated in the Act, was put in doubt within a few months of the new Northern Ireland Government taking office. To these uncertainties was added a growing doubt about the financial basis of the new government. There was doubt also about responsibility for maintenance of public order, and the administration did not at first command security forces on which it could wholly rely.

There was a large factor of social and religious conflict mixed up with the political violence. The deeply self-conscious divisions between Protestants and Roman Catholics penetrated nearly every field of social life and emerged in constant angry clashes of values, traditions and local customs. In the outcome, apart from open opposition, large sections of the community were organised to boycott the new government or to deny it any practical co-operation in even its most uncontroversial tasks.

At the same time there was a deteriorating economic situation as the wartime boom in both industry and agriculture began to decline and unemployment increased. This made a large and increasing contribution to the causes of unrest and social conflict.

The Government of Northern Ireland thus faced a very daunting situation with limited and often unreliable resources. It is not surprising that many believed that its prospects of survival were small. But, in the long view, the challenges which it faced, and the rapid accumulation of hard experience which was forced upon it, probably made the new administration a tougher and more resilient organism than it could possibly have been had it been founded among circumstances of enervating tranquillity. As it was, there was no department of the new government which was not forced by circumstances to bring itself to a high degree of testing.

The area for which the government was responsible was just over 5,000 square miles of very varied country, with 245 miles of sea coast and about 200 miles of undefended land frontier, beyond which lay a much larger and rather hostile neighbouring country then in a state of revolution. There had been no census of population since 1911, but an estimate made in 1924 put the population of Northern Ireland at 1,279,000. About one third of the people were Roman Catholics, the rest being Protestants, of whom the Presbyterians were the largest body. About a third of the population lived in the city of Belfast and in the immediately adjacent area.

The contrasting economic emphasis in Northern Ireland and in the south was shown by the fact that the 1911 census had recorded that 19.6 per cent of persons of twenty years and upwards in Northern Ireland were engaged in agriculture, while in the rest of Ireland the figure was 29.0 per cent, whereas the percentage engaged in industry in Northern Ireland had been 28.7, compared with only 15.5 per cent in the rest of Ireland.

Although industry appeared to offer prospects of wealth to Northern Ireland, the province had virtually no raw materials, no economically workable coal or iron. And some of the biggest industries, particularly shipbuilding and linen manufactures, were engaged in a type of production for which demand at that time was rapidly wilting.

The agriculture of Northern Ireland was backward compared with other parts of the British Isles. In 1924 it was recorded that 86 per cent of the 105,000 agricultural holdings were of less than fifty acres. This was the highest relative proportion of small farms to be found in any of the regions of the British Isles, including the rest of Ireland where the percentage had been 78.5 in 1917.

Significantly, Northern Ireland also had the highest death rate from tuberculosis in the British Isles and the highest infantile mortality rate outside Scotland.

Apart from these material and economic disadvantages, Northern Ireland suffered also from a certain bleakness, an indefinable poverty in the quality of life in terms of culture or of recognition of the cultural needs of the community. Belfast was in such respects an intensely provincial town. The centre had been elsewhere. When any foundation of a cultural nature had been established in Ireland, it had naturally been located in Dublin. Dublin had been the place for academies, art galleries, theatres and schools of music or art. Belfast had had its own university only since 1908, while Dublin had long had two universities. The result had been that, while Ulster certainly produced many people of creative talent in various fields, those people had tended to move away in order to seek elsewhere better educational facilities and a more encouraging and congenial background.

The 1911 census of population supplies a crude but significant index of a difference between life in Northern Ireland and life further south. At that time 3.5 per cent of the population of twenty years and upwards in the area now comprising Northern Ireland followed occupations classified as 'professional', while in the rest of Ireland the corresponding percentage was 5.1. In effect, among every two hundred adults in Southern Ireland there were ten who had professional education and qualifications but there were only seven of these among every two hundred adults in Northern Ireland.

It is thus not true, as is sometimes assumed, that Northern Ireland was a privileged area enjoying special advantages which it did not share with the rest of Ireland. Apart from its industries, which were at that time getting into a parlous state, the province was behind and inferior to the rest of Ireland in general prosperity, in agriculture, higher educational and cultural facilities, in public health and in a good many other respects.

The new government had thus more than a daunting range of immediate tasks to confront it. It also had, beyond these, a mass of arrears and handicaps inherited from the past. In many cases these were the result of a neglect which Ulster had suffered under the legislation of Westminster and the administration of Dublin Castle and Whitehall; for British governments in the nineteenth and early twentieth centuries had been deeply influenced by a laudable desire to remove adverse conditions in the southern and Roman Catholic areas of Ireland and had tended to take less interest in the north.

5. The Struggle for Survival

'It can safely be said that the great majority of those who were victims of these angry conflicts, those who were killed, wounded, terrorised or deprived of their worldly goods and of their homes, were people who had little or no moral responsibility for the conflicts in which they were caught up.'

The first concern of the Government of Northern Ireland was to stay alive. The very existence of the Ulster administration involved it in that bitter conflict which was going on in Ireland between the British Government and the republican organisation which claimed to be the true Government of Ireland.

The motto Sinn Fein—'we ourselves' or 'ourselves alone'—implied a claim to entire self-determination, without negotiation or concession. Having established this doctrine of legal and moral right, the young men who claimed to represent the Republic acted with great courage and dedication, but their acts and attitudes fell with extremely cruel effect upon large numbers of other people.

Having established their own doctrine and criterion of right and of loyalty, the republicans felt free to kill in its name. The first victims had been the police. Classified as uniformed agents of a foreign enemy with which the Republic was at war, many of them were individually shot or otherwise done to death, though most of them were at first unarmed and were fulfilling a purely civil function.

Beyond the police or the military the republicans found further targets in a desultory way in nearly any personnel or equipment that seemed to represent British administration in Ireland. Many of the buildings and institutions that were destroyed, such as co-operative dairies or isolated Protestant homes, had no connection with political objectives.

Many cruel effects of the work of republican activists sprang from the fact that they continually operated from among a civil population which was not fully committed to their cause. In Northern Ireland in particular this produced much suffering. Gunmen came to a district, did what they could to disrupt the normal machinery of civil life, using the inhabitants as a shield for their activities. Then they moved on, leaving their frequently far from willing hosts to suffer any reaction to what had happened. Arguing that he was at war and that in war all is fair, the roving republican gunman repudiated all responsibility for the repercussions that came from his acts. Taking a risk himself, he felt that he had a right to force others to do the same.

The effects of this upon town and country life were more socially destructive in Ulster than in any other part of Ireland; for the members of the Irish Republican Army worked invariably from within the Roman Catholic community which, in Ulster, though not elsewhere in Ireland, faced a powerful antithetical Protestant community.

While most Ulster Roman Catholics were certainly anti-Unionist, not by any means all of them were eager to lend themselves to the new southern republicanism. Most of them stood rather in the tradition of a more old-fashioned and largely constitutionalist nationalism. The acts of I.R.A. men, however, tended to identify the whole Roman Catholic community in the minds of many Protestant Unionists with the hostile and wholly alien republicanism of 1916 and Dail Eireann.

The Republican gunmen, too, were not politically discriminating in what they did. A frequent activity in Belfast was the posting of a sniper to fire from under the eaves of a house, and his victim was as likely to be a child or a bread roundsman or a chance passenger on a passing tramcar as anybody of the least military or political significance.

Inevitably the result of republican intervention in Northern Ireland was the building up of a vigorous reaction, involving reprisals of various kinds. In Dublin one never knew where some shooting incident might arise; but in Belfast there was a distinct and predictable geography for such things and this coincided closely with the geography of religious denomination in the city. An occasional incident might occur outside one of the predictable areas, but generally the dangerous districts were well known. Reprisals could therefore rather easily take the form of setting fire to houses. In areas of mixed religion the predominant religious group often evicted households of opposite religion, and agencies worked to arrange exchanges of homes for households which had found themselves living in or on the edge of a hostile district. Evictions were much more than reprisals. They were also security measures motivated by fear.

Another form of reaction was the exclusion from their place of work of the workers of one religious affiliation by those of another. Roman Catholics, for example, found themselves forcibly excluded from their jobs in the shipyards. This trend gained an enhanced significance from the fact that it occurred in a time of growing industrial depression and increasing unemployment; and in some trades the tension and difficulties were further increased by a boycott of Ulster goods organised throughout the south and west of Ireland. And through all this unrest there were sharp savage incidents of murder which each became powerfully counter-productive.

As in all such situations, it can safely be said that the great majority of those who were victims of these angry conflicts, those who were killed, wounded, terrorised or deprived of their worldly goods and of their homes, were people who had little or no moral responsibility for the conflicts in which they were caught up.

The Government of Ireland Act had reserved control of the police to the United Kingdom Government. Section 9(1) of the Act stated that 'the Royal Irish Constabulary and the Dublin Metropolitan Police . . . shall be reserved matters until such date, not being later than the expiration of three years after the appointed day, as His Majesty in Council may determine."

But the Royal Irish Constabulary were already in grave trouble and had suffered heavy casualties at the hands of the Republicans. There was a dangerous gap to be filled in Northern Ireland. The army could handle many duties, but there had to be a force based in the province itself, able to act both as a security force and as a civil police force. For this purpose there was established the Ulster Special Constabulary. Contrary to what is often believed, this force was not established by the Government of Northern Ireland, nor was it an extension of the Royal Ulster Constabulary. It was raised by the United Kingdom Government under the Special Constables (Ireland) Act of 1832, a piece of legislation which had actually preceded the Act of 1836 which established a unified regular police force in Ireland.

Recruiting for the Ulster Special Constabulary was opened on 1 November 1920 before the Government of Northern Ireland was set up and even before the Government of Ireland Act of 1920 had received the Royal Assent.

There were three classes into which enlistment could be made. Class A involved full-time service obligations, Class B involved part-time service, and Class C was a reserve liable to be called up in a grave emergency. The A Specials could be posted anywhere in Northern Ireland; but the B Specials served only in their own districts.

In the first year over 8,000 men joined the A Specials and 25,000 joined the B Specials. At the end of 1921, in the light of the developing situation, a further branch of the Specials was developed, the C1 Class. This was organised on semi-military lines and had an establishment of nearly 11,000 men. They were on a part-time service like the B Specials, but liable to call-up for full-time duty if required.

Many ex-servicemen served in the Specials and in particular a very high proportion of their officers had seen active fighting service. Prominent in organising the Special Constabulary in frontier areas was Captain Basil Brooke, the future Lord Brookeborough, later to be Prime Minister of Northern Ireland.

It was this force which ensured the security of Northern Ireland during the first perilous months and years of its existence. Most of the arms and equipment were old army material and their early uniforms were old army uniforms rather unsuccessfully dyed a darker colour. They are not to be confused with the 'Black and Tans', a force which did not operate in Northern Ireland.

In June 1922 The Royal Ulster Constabulary was founded under an Act of the Northern Ireland Parliament. Their number was limited by statute to 3,000. The Royal Irish Constabulary was disbanded, and 1,400 of its serving members joined the new force and provided the nucleus of its organisation.

The main work of the Specials and of the Royal Ulster Constabulary lay not so much in the occasional incidents of guerrilla warfare with infiltrating republican gunmen as in the protracted strategy of containment and prevention, the night watches, the innumerable checks, patrols and searches. But violent encounters did occur, and there were few people in the province who did not from time to time hear gunfire in the night and feel cause in other ways to fear the nervous trigger-happy atmosphere of those times.

It would not be possible here to provide a detailed narrative of 'the Troubles' which went on through the opening years of Northern Ireland's newly-won political identity. The extent and intensity of the violence which spread through the province was to a considerable degree affected by events in the South. Some of the ugliest and most bitterly remembered incidents occurred in the border counties.

Expressed statistically, the disturbances do not seem very extensive in terms of persons killed or wounded;

but it is necessary to recollect that they occurred in a small community. To get a notion of their impact upon Ulster, it might be useful to remember the relative sizes of populations and consider that it would be necessary to multiply all the figures by about thirty-five to bring them up to the population scale of Britain. Thus in 1922, altogether 232 people were known to have been killed in the strife in Northern Ireland, and nearly 1,000 people were wounded. And, in the money values of those times, over £3,000,000 worth of property was destroyed by fire or explosion. Many of the dead had been murdered because they had given information to the police. In addition to incidents of killing, wounding or burning, there were many cases of outrage of various kinds on persons or property, including a lot of cases of tarring and feathering and chaining to railings. The victims of this last form of outrage were mostly people who had given or were thought to have given information to the police. Now if all this had happened in Britain on a scale thirty-five times larger, with over 8,000 deaths and around 35,000 other casualties and over £100,000,000 of arson and bombing in the money values of the time, the impact upon the public mind and memory would have been considerable.

The pervasiveness of the trouble among a small population meant that there was hardly anybody in Northern Ireland who did not have his own disturbing story of something that happened quite close to him. The violence, too, was not something that ever came to a final end or resolution, like a war which could end with a peace settlemene. This violence has recurred at intervals over half a century and has remained endemic, activated from time to time from outside. Moreover, the social circumstances upon which these disasters made their impact, and the fact of their recurrence on a much smaller scale in later years, produced tragic social effects in deepening the differences between religious groups in the province. In practical terms, a Republican gunman, or anybody who sheltered or aided him or turned a blind eye on his activities, was sure to be a Roman Catholic; and any member of the Special Constabulary was sure to be a Protestant.

While it is difficult to secure a satisfactory analysis of how religious denomination took effect directly in the period of major conflict, it would appear that, once they were fully involved in rioting and conflict with one another, the two main religious groups in Northern Ireland each produced casualties in the opposite camp roughly proportionate to their own numbers. Thus during a bad three weeks in February 1922 when 138 casualties were reported, 96 of these were among Roman Catholics and 42 among Protestants. On the other hand, the event which particularly evoked bitterness that month is statistically excluded, for it took place outside Northern Ireland territory. A party of sixteen Special Constables were shot at close range by republicans as they sat in their train at Clones Station in the Irish Free State (later the Republic), Four were killed and eight wounded. The railway line in this area crossed the frontier at several points.

The year 1922 saw big fluctuations in the situation, arising from the changing events in the South. By the close of 1921 the Articles of Agreement had been signed between the United Kingdom Government and the republican leaders. For a short period in the spring, therefore, the Irish Republican Army was free to devote all its energies to attack and disruption in Northern Ireland. But, later in the same year, when the whole Republican movement was split over the acceptance or rejection of the terms of the 'Treaty', and civil war had developed in the south, the attacks on Ulster fell away. Yet the Unionist north remained an objective for attack from both sides in the southern civil war, since incursions into Northern Ireland continued to serve as an acceptable balm or catalyst for those engaged in southern strife. The civil war, therefore, kept overflowing the frontier in various forms.

The methods of action and organisation which the Northern Ireland Government used, as it took over the Special Constabulary and then a regular police force from the British Government, were those which the United Kingdom Government had been using in Ireland. Similarly they adopted the legal procedures which the United Kingdom Government had used to strengthen the hand of authority in dealing with subversion and violence. In the Civil Authorities (Special Powers) Act (Northern Ireland), 1922, the Northern Ireland Government gave itself the same powers which the British Government had used under the Defence of the Realm Consolidation Act of 1914 and the Restoration of Order in Ireland Act of 1920 and various regulations made under those Acts.

The Act of 1922 gave the Minister of Home Affairs for Northern Ireland considerable powers, most of which he could delegate to 'any officer of police'. These powers were no more extensive than the United Kingdom Government had already been exercising, nor were they of a kind unusual in any country where political violence has been rife. The Act gave the Minister power to make regulations, and a schedule to the Act set out a first series of these regulations. These he could withdraw or add to by Statutory Rules and Orders, to be laid before Parliament as soon as made. Powers conferred on the Minister in the original regulations included powers of search and arrest without warrant, appropriation of documents and other property, destruction of buildings, questioning of witnesses, banning of meetings and publications, prohibition of approach to special places. A later regulation gave the Minister power to make interment and exclusion orders.

The placing of this Act on a permanent footing in the face of later and continued trouble from the I.R.A. made it the subject of controversy; but it was not controversial in any way when it first went into operation as a temporary measure. In this connection, however, it ought to be noted that the original Act was only a starting point in the development of the law in Northern Ireland on special powers. A study of the text of the original Act would thus give an entirely false impression of the state of the law even a relatively short time after the passing of that Act, for many of the original regulations were withdrawn and some others issued. Many of the subjects dealt with came presently to be regulated by other Acts of quite a different kind, and parts of the Act were soon superseded. Some portions of it, and some of the regulations made under it, were never used. This was the case with a section which provided for the death penalty for certain offences relating to the possession and use of explosives.

6. The 1925 Agreement

'Here was an admirable agreement, reached in an atmosphere of great cordiality. It provided for peace and friendship in Ireland between north and south, for mutual recognition, mutual aid and extending mutual consultation and co-operation.'

While the struggle to restore peace and the rule of law went on in Northern Ireland, the whole Irish context of Northern Ireland's constitutional position was changing.

In the south and west of Ireland the power of the republicans was being restricted and broken by the forces of the Crown. There was now far less evidence of co-ordination or of central direction in republican activities. Unattached republican flying columns careered about the country in stolen cars and did very much as they pleased. In some cases roving gangs committed purposeless atrocities, including murders of retired policemen and soldiers and isolated Protestants. Yet on the Irish side in the conflict no force other than the republicans emerged to represent the community at large. The British government, therefore, opened negotiations with the republican leaders, and, at the close of 1921, Articles of Agreement were drawn up and signed. This is the document often referred to in Ireland as 'the Treaty'.

The main provisions of the Articles of Agreement gave Ireland the same constitutional status as Canada, what had come to be known as dominion status. It was to be called the Irish Free State. The powers of the government of the Irish Free State were not to be exercised over Northern Ireland for a month after the ratification of the Agreement by Parliament. If, before the end of that month, both Houses of Parliament of Northern Ireland should present an address to the King to that effect, the powers of the government of the Irish Free State were not to extend to Northern Ireland, and Northern Ireland was to be governed by the provisions of the Government of Ireland Act 1920, including the provisions with regard to the Council of Ireland.

At the earliest possible moment the parliament of Northern Ireland presented the necessary address to the King by which the province opted out of the Free State and remained within the United Kingdom under the terms of the Act of 1920.

This settlement was to set the pattern of political and constitutional relations in Ireland for the next half century. It is true that the Free State later became a republic outside the Commonwealth. But the general pattern remained, with an independent self-governing state comprising five-sixths of the island's surface and two-thirds of its population, with the remaining sixth of the island's area and a third of its population existing as a partly self-ruling province within the United Kingdom.

Although in the long view this was indeed a settlement that worked, its immediate effect for Northern Ireland was extremely unsettling. It threw into doubt three aspects of that earlier 1920 settlement which the majority in Northern Ireland had agreed to accept. It brought into question the frontier of Northern Ireland as defined in the Act of 1920. It put into doubt the financial relations which were to exist between Northern Ireland and the rest of the United Kingdom. And it raised in a new form the question of Northern Ireland's relationship with the rest of Ireland.

Of these three issues, it was naturally the frontier question which excited the greatest feeling and anxiety in Ulster. The reopening of the matter was felt to show bad faith on the part of the British government. That it was reopened at all was a concession to the republican side in the negotiations.

The form in which the frontier question was reopened was such as to make it a subject of burning controversy for several years. By the Articles of Agreement, if Northern Ireland chose to remain outside the Irish Free State, a commission of three people—one appointed by the Free State government, one by the government of Northern Ireland and one by the British government to act as chairman—'shall determine in accordance with the wishes of the inhabitants, so far as may be compatible with economic and geographical conditions, the boundaries between Northern Ireland and the rest of Ireland'.

Craig, as Prime Minister of Northern Ireland, was always open to the possibility of an understanding with the republicans. Generally he deplored their attitudes, not just because they were republicans but because he felt them to be totally unrealistic. In May 1921 he had gone to Dublin and entrusted himself to a republican escort who brought him to a secret meeting with the republican leader Eamonn De

Valera, but ninety minutes of talk, mostly by De Valera, brought no practical result. On later occasions Craig had discussions with Michael Collins both in London and in Dublin. From these discussions the best that emerged was an informal agreement that the boycott of Ulster goods which had been organised in the south should be relaxed and that efforts should be made to secure the release of Ulster people who had been kidnapped from the Border counties. But in no republican quarter could Craig find any easy possibility of securing an agreement to differ in a friendly spirit on political or territorial matters. Collins indeed seemed to envisage the cession to the Free State of a couple of Northern Ireland counties, with nothing given in return.

When the question of the frontier was thrown open again by the Articles of Agreement and by the legislation based upon them, which led to the formal establishment of the Irish Free State, and when no possible compromise emerged from discussions with Collins, Craig toured the frontier making speeches. He rejected firmly the idea of a boundary commission and used the slogans 'Not an inch' and 'What we have we hold'. He rallied to the support of this policy a large body of indignant public opinion in Ulster.

It is convenient here to anticipate events and describe the final outcome: but it has at the same time to be remembered that the Border question lay open for nearly four years, creating anger and ill will and leaving many people in doubt and anxiety as to their own future and the future of their property, their farming prospects, their business interests, their employment or the educational and employment future of their children.

Consistent with its policy of regarding the terms of the 1920 Act as final so far as the frontier was concerned, the Northern Ireland government refused to appoint a member to the three-man Boundary Commission. The United Kingdom government therefore obtained the passing of the necessary legislation to appoint a commissioner to represent Northern Ireland. The person thus appointed by the United Kingdom government was Mr. J. R. Fisher, editor of *The Northern Whig*, a Belfast daily newspaper with liberal and radical traditions and Unionist principles. The Free State was represented by Professor Eoin MacNeill, a prominent and respected figure of the republican movement, Minister of Education in the new Free State government, and an Ulsterman by birth. The chairman appointed by the British government was Mr. Justice Richard Feetham of South Africa. The commission was finally set up only in 1924.

The view of the Free State government was, in effect, that all the Commission had to do was to find out what parts of Northern Ireland could establish a claim to remain outside the control of that government. Enthusiastic republicans envisaged the cession to the Free State of all Tyrone and Fermanagh, most of Londonderry and large areas of Armagh and Down. Much depended upon the view taken of the functions of the commission by Mr. Justice Feetham, its chairman and also its legal expert. He held that the frontiers of Northern Ireland as established by the Act of 1920 were specifically recognised by the Articles of Agreement of 1921 and that all that the Commissioners were called upon to do was to determine adjustments to these frontiers where there was strong evidence of need. He did not accept the view that it was the business of the Commission to assign large areas of Northern Ireland to the Free State. He also held that it was as much the business of the Commissioners to determine transfers of territory from the Free State to Northern Ireland as from Northern Ireland to the Free State.

As the Commissioners proceeded with their work and heard representations from various interested parties, speculation ran wild. The Northern Ireland government, though rejecting the purpose of the Commission, did not put any obstacles in the way of its investigations and enquiries and indeed facilitated it in its work at ground level.

On 7 November 1925, the *Morning Post* created a major political sensation by publishing a map which was claimed to represent the boundary changes under consideration by the Commissioners. The map showed small cessions of territory from Northern Ireland to the Free State but also the cession of an area of Donegal from the Free State to Northern Ireland. The publication, 45 years later, of the report of the Commissioners, has substantially confirmed the accuracy of the 'leakage' which the *Morning Post* published in 1925. Professor MacNeill resigned both from the Commission and the Free State government, and the Commission, in effect, broke down.

This failure of the Boundary Commissioners to agree in presenting a final solution of the problem submitted to them convinced the Governments of the United Kingdom and of the Free State that they had been working on a fruitless project and that a fresh start was needed. The Free State government had gone through much tragic and chastening experience in a civil war with those who had once been colleagues and comrades in the republican movement. The British government and certainly the Northern Ireland government were both weary of the whole business.

A new spirit of relaxation and generosity began to manifest itself. In particular, W. T. Cosgrave, the head of the Free State government, and his cabinet colleagues, had come to realise that, if north and south were to draw together in Ireland, it could not be by niggling over small areas of territory or by engaging one another in any kind of legalistic argument. It must be by co-operation in an open and friendly spirit.

A conference was held in London and from it there emerged an agreement which provided for mutual recognition and co-operation between north and south. The agreement was a tripartite one, signed by representatives of the United Kingdom government, the government of the Irish Free State and the government of Northern Ireland.

The preamble to the agreement referred to the Articles of Agreement of 1921 and stated that 'the progress of events and the improved relations now subsisting between the British Government, the Government of the Irish Free State and the Government of Northern Ireland and their respective peoples' made it desirable 'to amend and supplement the said Articles of Agreement so as to avoid any causes of friction which might mar or retard the further growth of friendly relations between the said governments and people' and declared that the three governments were 'united in amity in this undertaking' and were 'resolved mutually to aid one another in a spirit of neighbourly comradeship'.

The agreement included certain adjustments of financial relations between the United Kingdom and the Free State; but the most important clauses concerned Northern Ireland. It was agreed to revoke the provisions of the Articles of Agreement of 1921 which led to the setting up of the Boundary Commission and to accept the territorial extent of Northern Ireland as being the area defined in the Government of Ireland Act, 1920. So the protracted friction over the Border question was brought to a close and the frontiers of Northern Ireland were left intact.

Another matter which was cleared up in the agreement was the Council of Ireland. This was the device embodied in the Act of 1920, and in the Articles of Agreement of 1921, for a sort of joint parliament of north and south. With the granting of dominion status to the Irish Free State, while Northern Ireland remained a province of the United Kingdom, the two parties who were to have met in this Council were no longer on an equal footing and no longer had indentical powers. It was now appreciated that in the altered circumstances the Council was not an effective or useful project, since the two governments participating in it could no longer do so on terms of equality.

The new agreement of 1925 therefore abandoned the plan for the Council and transferred to the parliament and government of Northern Ireland such powers as would have been exercised by the Council in relation to Northern Ireland. But it was also agreed that 'the governments of the Irish Free State and of Northern Ireland shall meet together as and when necessary for the purpose of considering matters of common interest arising out of or connected with the exercise and administration of' the range of powers which would have been exercised by the Council of Ireland. Here, then, was an admirable agreement, reached in an atmosphere of great cordiality. It provided for peace and friendship in Ireland between north and south, for mutual aid and extending mutual consultation and co-operation. It was what every sensible person wanted.

The agreement was received with enthusiasm in Northern Ireland. And in a Christmas letter from Cosgrave to Craig, the head of the Free State government referred to the good reception that it had had in the south. He wrote, 'The Agreement was, and is, regarded by a very large number of people here, including the professions and business classes, as the best contribution so far made by its signatories and their governments.' He added that 'the preamable touched people's hearts here in almost all cases'.

It seems entirely justifiable to attribute a great part of the more discouraging and occasionally tragic developments in Ireland in later years to the fact that the opportunities which the 1925 agreement threw open were not taken, that the agreement itself was not put effectively into operation in its more positive aspects, and that it was later dishonoured and disowned by one of the parties to it.

7. Divisions and Recession

'From the outset let us see that the Catholic minority have nothing to fear from the Protestant majority. Let us take care to win all that is best among those who have been opposed to us in the past. While maintaining intact our own religion, let us give the same rights to the religion of our neighbours.' Lord Carson.

The circumstances in which Northern Ireland had been established, and the tensions and conflicts of its opening years, had greatly heightened the self-consciousness of the denominational cleavage between Protestants and Roman Catholics. The identification of these religious groupings with political opinion had become much more rigid, and it had become much harder for individuals to cross the religious and political frontiers or ignore them.

Superficially viewed, this identification of politics with religion was arguably the outcome of several past centuries during which Protestantism had been identified with the conquerors, the rulers, the possessors and the privileged, while the Roman Catholic form of religion had been that of the conquered, the ruled, the dispossessed and the unprivileged. But this would be an inadequate explanation of the situation that had developed in Ulster; for the preceding years had seen much blurring of these social frontiers and many prominent people traversing them. There had been Roman Catholics who had sat in parliament as Unionists and there had been Protestants who had been leaders among Irish nationalists and republicans. There had also been many indications of the growth of a sense of community that transcended religious differences in various fields of social life. To give an example which will appeal to those who know Ulster well, the annual commemorative celebrations of the relief of Londonderry after the siege of 1689, which in the twentieth century have been an exclusively Protestant event, had been attended back in the nineteenth century by the local Roman Catholic bishop. In fact the position which confronted government and people alike in Northern Ireland with regard to the religious groups in the province was not simply a development from the past. It was a grave deterioration from the past. There is no one simple explanation of this deterioration; but the use which republican terrorists had made of the Roman Catholic community as a cover and a medium for their activities in Northern Ireland was a major contributory factor.

At the same time the Protestant element in Unionism had been greatly strengthened by nearly forty years of crisis during which the Ulster Protestants, with their position threatened as citizens of the United Kingdom, had been a frightened minority in Ireland. Unionism, in its desperate sense of urgency during those years, could neglect no ally. One of its most important sources of support came to be the Orange Institution, a Protestant organisation which had suffered many vicissitudes since its founding in 1795 after a violent riot in Co. Armagh. When the crisis of Unionism began in the 1880's, this body was in rather a run-down condition; but it was quickly seized upon by Unionists as a ready-made instrument and given a new and improved quality and a fresh lease of life.

Since that rejuvenation of the Orange Order it has come to be much more than an organisation to promote the interests of Protestantism. It plays an important social function in town and country. Its halls serve as meeting places for a much wider range of gatherings than those which are strictly its own, providing a venue for dances, concerts, cookery demonstrations, flower shows, meetings of young farmers and many other activities which are concerned with the general life of the community.

Each member of the Orange Order is required, as a qualification for membership, to lead a moral life, observe his country's laws and, in asserting his Protestant principles, to abstain 'from all uncharitable words, actions or sentiments towards his Roman Catholic brethren.' Commitment to reiterated principles does have its influence, even if it is not as deep an influence as some would like to claim. The Order has served to give a restrained and disciplined expression to forces in Ulster which might have been very destructive if they had not to some extent been canalised and controlled. Its membership in Northern Ireland has usually been estimated at about 100,000. If to this actual membership one adds a margin of sympathisers connected by family and other ties to the actual members, the Orange body might represent fairly directly as many as 300,000 people. No political party forming a government in Northern Ireland could neglect or alienate such a substantial body of opinion. Yet the association of the government with such a powerful denominational pressure group and interest was bound to cut that government off from support or sympathy that might have developed among the religious minority in the province. An Ulster Roman Catholic might be in sympathy with the Union and might prefer to vote Unionist, but he was unlikely to want to vote for an Orangeman.

The actions of southern republicans had also placed the Roman Catholic community in Northern Ireland from the outset in a position of great disadvantage and isolation. Largely involuntarily, it became identified in the eyes of the Protestants with the policy of physical force as expressed by Sinn Féin and the Irish Republican Army (I.R.A.). As a result it had to face an exasperated and outraged Protestant majority. Some of its members were led into further difficulties by believing too readily a vigorous propaganda coming mainly from the south to the effect that the Northern Ireland government could not long survive and might usefully be boycotted and denied any form of co-operation. One of the severest distresses of the Ulster Roman Catholic community was that events repeatedly emphasised their isolation by showing them that, in circumstances and interests, they were by no means homogeneous with their co-religionists in the rest of Ireland.

The leaders of the new government were well aware of the acute difficulties of the minority in the province and anxious to promote reconciliation. In a message to the Unionists of Ulster, Carson, their former leader, wrote in 1921, 'From the outset let us see that the Catholic minority have nothing to fear from the Protestant majority. Let us take care to win all that is best among those who have been opposed to us in the past. While maintaining intact our own religion, let us give the same rights to the religion of our neighbours'. In the Northern Ireland parliament, Craig spoke reassuringly and with undoubted sincerity of the government's firm intention to see that justice was done to every member of the community. The Orangemen at their annual gathering in 1922 adopted a resolution declaring that they stood 'for equal rights, equal liberties and equal opportunities for all men, no matter what their religious outlook and no matter what their political bias.' Yet in the circumstances of the period it was perhaps not surprising that on the Roman Catholic side the response was negative. No Roman Catholic elected to the Northern Ireland parliament at first attended its sessions. Members of the Roman Catholic hierarchy attended no state functions. When some Roman Catholic members began to attend parliament in 1925, the Speaker of the House of Commons invited the Archbishop of Armagh, Cardinal O'Donnell, to nominate a chaplain to parliament, as had been done by such Protestant religious bodies as had members in parliament, but no such chaplain was appointed until the year 1971.

In February, 1922, Roman Catholic teachers in Co. Tyrone met and expressed their objection to education in the province falling under the control of the parliament of Northern Ireland. They called upon the provisional government of the Irish Free State to administer and finance Roman Catholic education in Northern Ireland and pledged themselves not to accept their salaries from the Northern Ireland government. The managers and staffs of many Roman Catholic schools tried to adopt a policy more or less on these lines. The Northern Ireland government appointed a Roman Catholic as permanent secretary to the Ministry of Education, paid grants and salaries to all who would accept them and held them available for those who would not, did nothing to embarrass any who had placed themselves in any difficult position, and gradually restored administrative normality.

In the police the policy was adopted of reserving one-third of all the places in the force for Roman Catholics; but most of these places found no applicants. Some Roman Catholics did nevertheless join the police and also—one might say, even—the Special Constabulary. This fortunate if too limited trend was helped by the fact that the Royal Ulster Constabulary carried on both the traditions and some of the members of the old Royal Irish Constabulary. In the civil service there was also for a long time only a small degree of interest by Roman Catholics. In judicial appointments the government also tried to give a fair proportion of opportunity to the religious minority, and the first Lord Chief Justice of Northern Ireland was a Roman Catholic.

While the government tried to pursue these principles of giving jobs fairly without regard to religious affiliations, it was much harder to secure a satisfactory application of such principles in some areas in local government and in some forms of private employment. During the more troubled times a large number of Roman Catholics had been forced out of their jobs. One of the advantages which Craig tried to draw from agreement with Michael Collins about the ending of the southern boycott of Ulster products and the release of kidnapped persons was that these concessions put him in a better position to persuade the Protestant shipyard workers of Belfast to let their Roman Catholic fellow workers come back to their jobs. In this, after personal negotiations, he had substantial success. But the general situation was deeply discouraging for a number of years and many left the province. The restoration of normality was also delayed by recurrent incidents of violence promoted by the I.R.A. It was not until 1930 that the persistent underground remnant of this body had to withdraw across the frontier, and in 1931 it was banned in the Free State as an unlawful association.

The task of promoting toleration and peace in the community was rendered much harder by the serious recession in industry which caused heavy unemployment. Statistics from the major Ulster industries in the 1920s tell a tale of shrinkage and decline. A shipbuilding industry, which in 1919 launched 134,456 net tonnage of shipping, launched a tonnage of 34,167 in 1925. The great Ulster linen industry was not only suffering from a sharp fall in demand and a swing to cheaper and less durable fabrics, but it had got into grave difficulties through lack of modernisation and through heavy capital investment in uneconomic forms of expansion to meet the production demands of wartime. Agriculture was not doing too badly and the Ministry of Agriculture could boast that, in 1925, 31.7 per cent of the total area of Northern Ireland was under crops, compared with 22.2 per cent of the total area of the Free State. But the wartime production boom had left some impoverishment of land from excessive flax cropping; and there was a slight but steady annual fall in the province's livestock population.

The compilation of trade figures for the province was beginning, but at first the only details available were of seaborne trade. Later these trade figures were to give a fuller picture of the province's economic life than is available for any other area of similarly small size in the United Kingdom and were to display an immense concentration of productive activity. But in the 1920s the figures showed only a slight annual downward creep in exports and a small upward creep of imports. In 1924 seaborne imports were worth £58,911,000 and exports £57,801,000.

The new frontiers were not at first at all a serious economic barrier, only an administrative frontier; but the very existence of a frontier and the circumstances of the times made it hard for any Northern Ireland business enterprise to function across it. In particular many businesses in the city of Londonderry lost their Donegal hinterland. The secession of the Free State from the United Kingdom was thus quite a severe blow to many shops, supply businesses and distributive trades in Northern Ireland.

It is not easy to give an exact picture of the unemployment situation in the province in those early years. The systems of insurance and classification have changed so much as to make comparison between unemployment totals at different periods unrealistic. Totals of unemployed in different years have to be related not to each other but rather to the totals of insured persons at the respective times. Thus July, 1923, saw 253,820 persons insured and an average for the year of 45,193 of them unemployed, showing that in the insured categories one person in five or six was at that time normally without work. In 1925 there was an average of 58,972 unemployed and there were 268,780 insured persons, showing a still higher rate of unemployment—one in every four or five insured people. With this it is necessary to take into account a presumptive high rate of unemployment among uninsured people and also the fact that there were much less adequate standards of relief and assistance than have since become available.

There was also a shortage of living accommodation and heavy arrears of house-building and replacement which had accumulated during the war years. There was a wide prevalence of poverty, malnutrition, overcrowding and disease. There were high rates of infant and maternal mortality and a high tuberculosis death rate.

The two parallel factors of strife in the community and recession in the economy tended to react adversely upon one another. When there was a shortage of employment there was a heightened tendency for Protestants and Roman Catholics to exclude one another from such businesses as they controlled or influenced. When economic pressure became allied with the deep divisions in the community it was perhaps understandable, if regrettable, that people with jobs to fill should tend to give them to their own 'sort' or for majority groups in industries to want to claim the whole shop floor for their co-politicals and co-religionists. A certain easy-going and good-natured tolerance and generosity which had sometimes appeared in such matters at an earlier period had now withered away.

In most areas, though certainly not in all, the local majority was Protestant. There was a long gap between the census of population taken in 1911 and the next one taken in 1926. The total population had changed little in those fifteen years, from 1,250,531 to 1,256,561; but, although Roman Catholics have tended to increase more rapidly than the total population in Northern Ireland, their numbers fell during this period by nearly 10,000, and from being 34.4 per cent of the population in 1911 they had become 33.5 per cent in 1926. This slight diminution in their numbers was probably largely the result of emigration prompted by the hardships and discouragements which they had suffered in those times.

There is one interpretation of these events which is sometimes propounded. It is suggested, on more or less Marxist principles, that the exacerbation of religious strife was a device used by capitalists and employers in Northern Ireland to divide and weaken labour. One can only say that there seems to be a great lack of supporting evidence for this thesis. On the contrary the larger industrial organisations operating in the province always tended to treat religious competition as a nuisance to be discouraged. In many cases they have intervened where they could to cool down feelings and remove or adjust causes of contention. In larger concerns appointments and promotions have gone to those judged to be best qualified quite regardless of religious affiliations. This is also true of enterprises under the government.

Many small businesses, on the other hand, particularly those that are largely family businesses, have always been run on quite candidly denominational lines. Thus in Belfast a high proportion of certain retail trading establishments are operated by Roman Catholics,—public houses, fruit shops, hairdressing and catering establishments, hotels—while in other businesses which serve the public—hardware, light engineering, furnishing, insurance broking and many more—Protestant operators are more numerous. Often a consciousness that a particular small business is of one religious affiliation while serving customers of another makes for good will.

But it was only after the middle 1920s that the mass of people in Northern Ireland began to be more at ease with one another as neighbours across the old dividing lines. And the peace was sometimes brittle and rather self-consciously maintained because under its surface many memories were still deeply scarred by shocking and unforgivable things.

Pictorial Section

		Page
1.	Government and Parliament	Thirty-Four
2.	Personalities	Forty-Six
3.	Historic Moments	Fifty-Six
4.	The Restless Years	Seventy
5.	War	Eighty
6.	Construction	Ninety-Two
7.	Industry and Agriculture	One Hundred & Two
8.	Education	One Hundred & Sixteen
9.	The Arts	One Hundred & Twenty-Six
10.	Sport	One Hundred & Thirty-Six
11.	Scenic	One Hundred & Forty-Six
12.	Transport, Tradition, Ulster American Links, Gracious Homes	One Hundred & Fifty-Eight

Government and Parliament

Pages Thirty-Four to Forty-Five

The scene at the first meeting of the Northern Ireland Parliament held in the City Hall, Belfast, on 7th June, 1921, when the Speaker —Sir Hugh O'Neill (now Lord Rathcavan) was elected.

Above right: King George V and Queen Mary drive to Belfast City Hall for the State Opening of the first Northern Ireland Parliament on 22nd June, 1921.

Right: King George V inspects the guard of honour mounted by the 1st Battalion Royal Ulster Rifles at the opening of Parliament.

Above left: Photograph of the State Opening of the first Parliament as King George V addresses Members and Senators.

Left: The first Northern Ireland Cabinet in session with Sir James Craig, the Prime Minister (later Lord Craigavon), in the chair. From left are: Mr. E. M. Archdale, Minister of Agriculture; Sir Dawson Bates, Minister of Home Affairs; Lord Londonderry, Minister of Education; Mr. H. M. Pollock, Minister of Finance; and Mr. J. M. Andrews, Minister of Labour.

Above: RAF aircraft fly overhead in salute at the laying of the foundation stone of the Northern Ireland Parliament Buildings in 1928.

Right: The Prince of Wales (later the Duke of Windsor), after opening the Northern Ireland Parliament Buildings on November 16, 1932.

Left: The main entrance to the Northern Ireland Parliament Buildings at Stormont. The building, in the Greek classical style, was designed by Sir Arnold Thomley.

Above: The Assembly Buildings in which the Parliament of Northern Ireland conducted its business until the opening of the Stormont buildings.

Below: A Cabinet of Lord Brookeborough (centre) in the late 50's. On the left (from left) are: Lieut.-Col. A. R. G. Gordon, Mr. John Andrews, Rev. Robert Moore, Captain Terence O'Neill. On the right (from right) are the Lord Glentoran, Mr. Morris May, Mr. Ivan Neill, Col. W. W. B. Topping. Seated behind Lord Brookeborough are Sir Arthur Kelly, Secretary to the Cabinet, and Mr. (later Sir Cecil) Cecil Bateman, Assistant Secretary.

Above: A Cabinet of Captain Terence O'Neill, Prime Minister 1963–1969: (From left to right): Front row: Mr. W. J. Morgan, Captain O'Neill, Mr. Brian Faulkner. Centre row: Mr. H. V. Kirk, Captain W. J. Long, Mr. William Craig. Back row: Mr. W. K. Fitzsimmons, Major J. D. Chichester-Clark, Mr. Brian McConnell and Mr. John Andrews.

Above: The administration of Major James Chichester-Clark after he succeeded Captain Terence O'Neill in 1969. From the left are: Mr. Roy Bradford, Minister of Commerce; Mr. R. W. Porter, Q.C., Minister of Home Affairs; Mr. Brian Faulkner, Minister of Development; Mr. J. L. O. Andrews, Minister in the Senate; Mr. William Fitzsimmons, Minister of Health and Social Services; Mr. H. V. Kirk, Minister of Finance; Mr. Phelim O'Neill, Minister of Agriculture; the Prime Minister; Mr. John Dobson, Leader of the House of Commons; Captain W. J. Long, Minister of Education; and Mr. Nat Minford, Minister of State, Ministry of Development.

Left: The administration of Mr. Brian Faulkner, when he became Prime Minister in 1971. The Rt. Hon. H. W. West, M.P. (Minister of Agriculture); the Rt. Hon. N. O. Minford, M.P. (Leader of the House of Commons and Minister of State at the Ministry of Development); Capt. the Rt. Hon. W. J. Long, J.P., M.P. (Minister of Education); the Rt. Hon. R. J. Bailie LL.B., M.P. (Minister of Commerce); Senator the Rt. Hon. J. L. O. Andrews D.L. (Minister in the Senate); Capt. the Rt. Hon. J. W. Brooke, D.L., M.P. (Minister of State at the Ministry of Finance and Chief Whip); the Rt. Hon. A. B. D. Faulkner, D.L., M.P. (Prime Minister); the Rt. Hon. R. H. Bradford, B.A., M.P. (Minister of Development); the Rt. Hon. H. V. Kirk, B.Com.Sc., F.C.A., J.P., M.P. (Minister of Finance); the Rt. Hon. W. K. Fitzsimmons, M.R.S.H., J.P., M.P. (Minister of Health and Social Services); the Rt. Hon. D. W. Bleakley, M.A., Dip.Econ. (Minister of Community Relations).

There have been five Governors of Northern Ireland, including Lord Grey of Naunton, the present Governor (left). His predecessors (above from left) were: the Duke of Abercorn 1921–45; the Earl Granville 1945–52; Lord Wakehurst 1952–64; Lord Erskine of Rerrick 1964–68.

Right: Government House, Hillsborough, Co. Down, official residence of the Governor of Northern Ireland since 1924. It was formerly the home of the Marquis of Downshire.

Personalities

Pages Forty-Six to Fifty-Five

NORTHERN IRELAND'S SIX PRIME MINISTERS

Above: Lord Craigavon, 1921-1940.

Below: Capt. Terence O'Neill (later Lord O'Neill), 1963-1969.

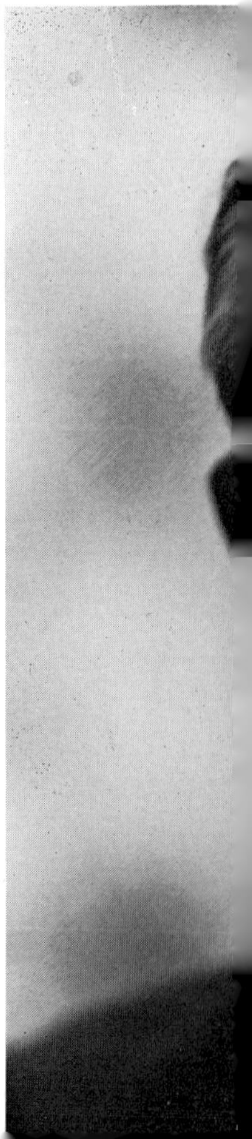

Above: Mr. John M. Andrews, 1940-43.

Above: Lord Brookeborough, 1943-1963.

Below: Major James D. Chichester-Clark, 1969–1971.

Mr. Brian Faulkner, 1971-

Lord and Lady Carson on one of their visits to Northern Ireland after the setting up of the new Parliament.

Above: Mr. Joe Devlin, M.P., leader of the Nationalist Opposition in Northern Ireland's first Parliament. He died in 1934 after a distinguished Parliamentary career.

Above: Mr. Eamonn De Valera, who became President of the Irish Republic in 1959. He is seen being put on board a south-bound train in 1924 after contravening an order forbidding him to enter Northern Ireland. The order was revoked in 1933. He was a member of the Northern Ireland Commons for Down and later South Down 1921–1938, but never took his seat.

Left: Mr. Cahir Healy who became "father" of the Northern Ireland House of Commons. He died in 1970, aged 93, and had been an M.P. at Westminster and Stormont for more than 50 years.

Below left: Mr. Jack Beattie, a Member of Parliament at both Stormont and Westminster.

Below right: Mr. Tommy Henderson, Independent M.P., who held the record for the longest speech ever made in the Northern Ireland Commons—it lasted $9\frac{1}{2}$ hours. He died in 1970.

Above: Major Maynard Sinclair, who was Minister of Finance and Deputy Prime Minister when he lost his life in the Princess Victoria disaster in 1953. He joined the Cabinet in 1943.

Above: Mr. William Grant, Minister of Health, 1944-1949, who introduced the National Health and Welfare legislation.

Right: Mr. Eddie McAteer, Leader of the first official Nationalist Opposition in the Northern Ireland House of Commons. He lost his seat in the 1969 general election.

Above: Mr. Robert Getgood, Trade Union organiser and Northern Ireland Labour M.P., 1945-1949.

Above: Mr. Harry Diamond, Republican Labour M.P. for Falls in the Northern Ireland Parliament 1945-1969.

Left: Mr. Harry Midgley, Labour M.P., who left the Opposition benches to become a member of the Northern Ireland Government. He was Minister of Education

Above: Dame Dehra Parker, first woman to become a member of the Northern Ireland Cabinet. She was Minister of Health and Local Government 1949-1957.

Above: Mr. Tom Boyd, formerly Leader of the Northern Ireland Labour Party.

Above: Mr. Gerard Fitt, Social Democratic and Labour Party, leader of the biggest Opposition party in the Northern Ireland House of Commons. He also sits as member for West Belfast at Westminster.

Above: Mr. John Hume, who defeated Mr. Eddie McAteer in the 1969 Northern Ireland general election. He came into prominence as one of the civil rights leaders in Londonderry.

Right: Mr. Ivan Cooper, elected Independent M.P. for mid-Derry in the Northern Ireland Commons in 1969. Mr. Cooper was also prominent in the Civil Rights campaign in Londonderry.

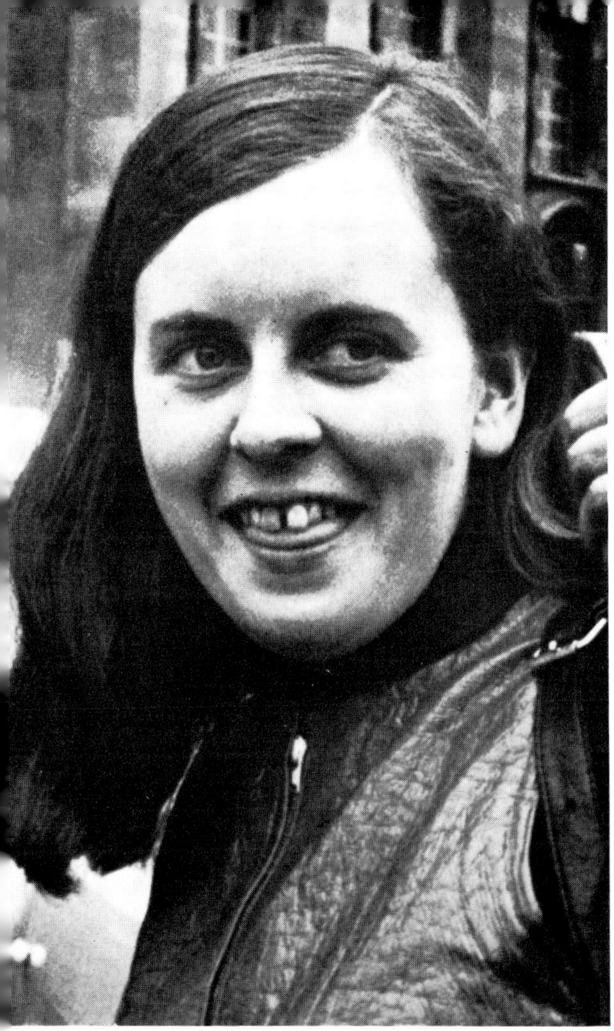

Left: Miss Bernadette Devlin, Independent member for Mid-Ulster at Westminster and prominent in the Civil Rights organisation.

Above: Rev. Ian Paisley who won the Bannside seat as a Protestant Unionist in the Northern Ireland Parliament in a by-election in 1970 following the resignation of Lord O'Neill. He was also elected as member for North Antrim at Westminster in the same year.

Left: Mr. Roderick O'Connor, leader of the Nationalist Party in the House of Commons.

Dated this 3rd day of December, 1925.

Signed on behalf of the British Government.

Stanley Baldwin.

Winston S. Churchill

Birkenhead

Signed on behalf of the Government of the Irish Free State.

Kevin O'Higgins

Signed on behalf of the Government of Northern Ireland.

James Craig.

Charles H. Blackmore

Secretary to the Cabinet of Northern Ireland.

Historic Moments

Pages Fifty-Six to Sixty-Nine

Above

Members of the House of Commons.

First Parliament of Northern Ireland, June, 1921

Front Row: Mrs. McMordie, Dr. H. S. Morrison, Rt. Hon R. Best, Capt. H. Dixon, Rt. Hon. H. M. Pollock, Rt. Hon. Sir James Craig, Rt. Hon R. W. H. O'Neill, Rt. Hon. E. M. Archdale, Rt. Hon. Sir R. Dawson Bates, Thomas Moles, Rt. Hon. J. M. Andrews, Sir Robert Anderson, Mrs. Dehra Chichester.

2nd Row: J. F. Gordon, R. J. Lynn, G. B. Hanna, J. H. Robb, J. M. Mark, Capt. the Honfl H. G. H. Mulholland, Dr. J. Campbell, S. McGuffiin, T. R. Lavery, J. Milne Barbour, R. D. Megaw, R. J. McKeown, Sir Crawford McCullagh, T. W. McMullan.

Back Row: Major D. G. Shillington, J. Cooper, J. A. Duff, Lloyd Campbell, Thompson Donald, R. J. Johnstone, F.R.C.S., W. T. Millar, W. Coote, W. J. Twaddell, T. H. Burn, R. McBride, W. Grant, R. Crawford.

Left and below: The 1925 Agreement and the

Government of Ireland Act, 1920.

[10 & 11 Geo. 5. Ch. 67.]

A.D. 1920.

ARRANGEMENT OF SECTIONS.

ESTABLISHMENT OF PARLIAMENTS FOR SOUTHERN IRELAND AND NORTHERN IRELAND AND A COUNCIL OF IRELAND.

Section.

1. Establishment of Parliaments of Southern and Northern Ireland.
2. Constitution of Council of Ireland.

POWER TO ESTABLISH A PARLIAMENT FOR THE WHOLE OF IRELAND.

3. Power to establish a Parliament for the whole of Ireland.

LEGISLATIVE POWERS.

4. Legislative powers of Irish Parliaments.
5. Prohibition of laws interfering with religious equality, taking property without compensation, &c.
6. Conflict of laws.
7. Powers of Council of Ireland to make orders respecting private Bill legislation for whole of Ireland.

EXECUTIVE AUTHORITY.

8. Executive powers.
9. Reserved matters.
10. Powers of Council of Ireland.

PROVISIONS AS TO PARLIAMENTS OF SOUTHERN AND NORTHERN IRELAND.

11. Summoning, &c., of Parliaments.
12. Royal assent to Bills.
13. Constitution of Senates.
14. Constitution of the Parliaments.
15. Application of election laws.

i

Above right: The Government of Ireland Act 1920, which really embodies the Constitution of Northern Ireland.

Right: Mr. W. F. Massey, Ulster born Prime Minister of New Zealand, at a students' rag in the grounds of Queen's University, Belfast, after he received the honorary degree of Doctor of Law in 1923.

Above: Mr. Ramsay MacDonald, Labour Prime Minister, with Sir James Craig and Mr. William Cosgrave, head of the Irish Free State Government, photographed at a meeting at Chequers in 1924 which was called at Mr. MacDonald's request to discuss Irish problems.

[15 & 16 GEO. 5.] *Ireland (Confirmation of Agreement) Act, 1925.* [CH. 77.]

CHAPTER 77.

An Act to confirm and give effect to a certain Agreement amending and supplementing the Articles of Agreement for a Treaty between Great Britain and Ireland to which the force of law was given by the Irish Free State (Agreement) Act, 1922, and by the Constitution of the Irish Free State (Saorstat Eireann) Act, 1922. A.D. 1925.

[10th December 1925.]

BE it enacted by the King's most Excellent Majesty, by and with the advice and consent of the Lords Spiritual and Temporal, and Commons, in this present Parliament assembled, and by the authority of the same, as follows:—

1.—(1) The Agreement set forth in the Schedule to this Act, being an Agreement amending and supplementing the Articles of Agreement for a Treaty between Great Britain and Ireland, to which the force of law was given by the Irish Free State (Agreement) Act, 1922, and by the Constitution of the Irish Free State (Saorstat Eireann) Act, 1922; is hereby confirmed, and the said Articles of Agreement for a Treaty and the Irish Free State (Agreement) Act, 1922, shall have effect accordingly. Confirmation of Agreement. 12 Geo. 5. c. 4.

(2) The date as from which the powers in relation to Northern Ireland, which by the Government of Ireland Act, 1920, are made powers of the Council of Ireland, are to be transferred to the Parliament and Government of Northern Ireland, shall be the first day of April,

Left and below: The 1925 Agreement and the signatories thereto.

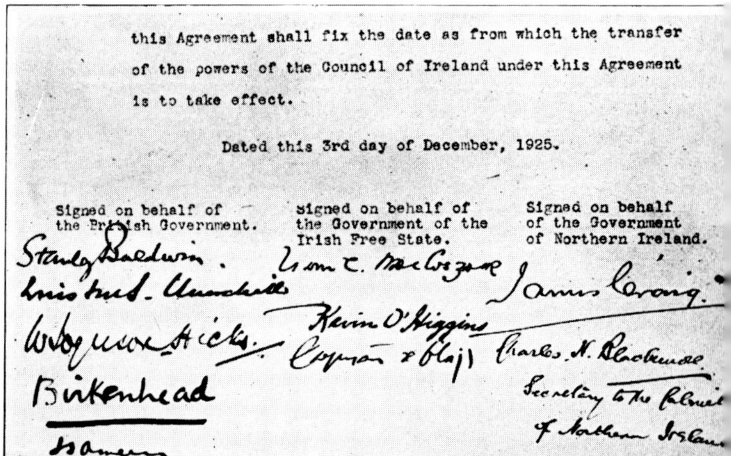
this Agreement shall fix the date as from which the transfer of the powers of the Council of Ireland under this Agreement is to take effect.

Dated this 3rd day of December, 1925.

Signed on behalf of the British Government.	Signed on behalf of the Government of the Irish Free State.	Signed on behalf of the Government of Northern Ireland.
Stanley Baldwin		James Craig
	Kevin O'Higgins	Charles H. Blackmore
Birkenhead		Secretary to the Cabinet of Northern Ireland

Below: Sir Denis Henry, first Lord Chief Justice of Northern Ireland, who died in 1925.

Right: The first woman to fly the Atlantic alone—Miss Amelia Earhart and her plane at Culmore, near Londonderry, where she made a forced landing in 1932.

Below: A seat on a jaunting car for Mr. Winston Churchill during a students' rag at Queen's University in 1926.

Above: Scene at the funeral of Lord Carson on October 29, 1935. The procession is shown in Royal Avenue on its way to Belfast Cathedral.

Below: The Duke of Abercorn, first Governor of Northern Ireland, at Stormont in January, 1936.

Inventor of the Ferguson tractor was Mr. Harry Ferguson who was born in Co. Down in 1884. He also won fame as an aviation pioneer, being the first Irishman to build and fly his own aeroplane.

The Duke of Kent, who was killed on active service, is seen with Sir James Andrews, Lord Chief Justice, after a visit to the Royal Courts of Justice in October, 1940.

Below: The funeral of Lord Craigavon, who died on November 24, 1940, passes the Carson statue in the grounds of Parliament Buildings. Lord Craigavon's burial place is at the east side of the Buildings.

General Eisenhower, Supreme Allied Commander in World War II, who received the freedom of Belfast in 1945. He is shown in front of the Northern Ireland Parliament Buildings during a visit to Stormont.

Field Marshal Viscount Montgomery inspects a guard of honour while visiting Long Kesh Aerodrome, (Co. Fermanagh) war-time R.A.F. base.

The Queen, then Princess Elizabeth, meets members of the A.T.S. during a visit to Northern Ireland in 1945.

(2) It is hereby declared that Northern Ireland remains part of His Majesty's dominions and of the United Kingdom and it is hereby affirmed that in no event will Northern Ireland or any part thereof cease to be part of His Majesty's dominions and of the United Kingdom without the consent of the Parliament of Northern Ireland.

Above and right: The Ireland Act of 1949 and the Clause which, for the first time, vested the destiny of Northern Ireland in its own Parliament.

12 & 13 GEO. 6 *Ireland Act*, 1949 CH. **41**

CHAPTER 41

An Act to recognise and declare the constitutional position as to the part of Ireland heretofore known as Eire, and to make provision as to the name by which it may be known and the manner in which the law is to apply in relation to it; to declare and affirm the constitutional position and the territorial integrity of Northern Ireland and to amend, as respects the Parliament of the United Kingdom, the law relating to the qualifications of electors in constituencies in Northern Ireland; and for purposes connected with the matters aforesaid.

[2nd June 1949]

BE it enacted by the King's most Excellent Majesty, by and with the advice and consent of the Lords Spiritual and Temporal, and Commons, in this present Parliament assembled, and by the authority of the same, as follows:—

1.—(1) It is hereby recognized and declared that the part of Ireland heretofore known as Eire ceased, as from the eighteenth day of April, nineteen hundred and forty-nine, to be part of His Majesty's dominions. **Constitutional provisions.**

(2) It is hereby declared that Northern Ireland remains part of His Majesty's dominions and of the United Kingdom and it is hereby affirmed that in no event will Northern Ireland or any part thereof cease to be part of His Majesty's dominions and of the United Kingdom without the consent of the Parliament of Northern Ireland.

(3) The part of Ireland referred to in subsection (1) of this section is hereafter in this Act referred to, and may in any Act, enactment or instrument passed or made after the passing of this Act be referred to, by the name attributed thereto by the law thereof, that is to say, as the Republic of Ireland.

Below: The aircraft ejector seat, which has saved the lives of hundreds of airmen since it became operational in 1948, was invented by Mr. James Martin who was born in Crossgar, Co. Down.

Above: The ill-fated Princess Victoria, which foundered in a gale near the Copeland Islands with the loss of 128 lives.

Right: A crowd waits outside the *Belfast Telegraph* on Sunday, February 1, 1953, for a special edition on the disaster.

Below: Sir Winston Churchill with four of the great soldiers of Ulster origin at the Mansion House, London, in 1955. On his left are Field Marshal Viscount Alanbrooke, Field Marshal Earl Alexander, and Field Marshal Sir Gerald Templer. On his right are Field Marshal Viscount Montgomery and Lord Brookeborough, then Prime Minister of Northern Ireland.

Above: After his period as U.S. President, General Eisenhower paid a visit to Northern Ireland in 1962 and is seen looking at the pillar erected in front of Belfast City Hall to mark the landing in Ulster of the first U.S. troops in Europe in 1942.

Left: Captain Terence O'Neill, then Prime Minister of Northern Ireland (now Lord O'Neill of the Maine) photographed with President Lyndon B. Johnson in the White House in 1964.

Above: The visit to Stormont in January, 1965, of Mr. Sean Lemass, Prime Minister of the Irish Republic, at the invitation of Captain Terence O'Neill, then Northern Ireland Prime Minister. They are shown at the entrance to Stormont Castle.

Above: Mr. Jack Lynch, who succeeded Mr. Lemass as Prime Minister of the Irish Republic in 1967, is greeted on a visit to Stormont by Captain Terence O'Neill and Mrs. O'Neill and members of the Cabinet.

Above: Cardinal Conway, the first Belfast man to be created a Cardinal of the Roman Catholic Church. Born in Dover Street, off the Falls Road, he is seen acknowledging a tumultous reception from a crowd outside St. Peter's Pro-Cathedral, Belfast.

Right: Mr. Sandy Scott, trade unionist, a leading figure in the highly successful efforts to maintain the peace in the Belfast shipyards at a critical period of unrest in 1969. He was subsequently awarded the M.B.E.

Above are shown a Maltese cross and one of a set of ninth century gold medallions found in the Girona.

Left: Robert Stenuit, Belgian underwater explorer, and his colleagues examining treasure they recovered from the Spanish Armada ship 'Girona', which sank off the North Antrim Coast nearly four hundred years ago.

IRELANDS LARGEST

The Restless Years

Pages Seventy to Seventy-Nine

Above: Troops and police search for a sniper in debris-covered Little George's Street during the Belfast troubles of the early 1920's.

Above: A military barricade at the corner of North Street and Upper Library Street during the Belfast disturbances of 1922.

Below: A crowd of people in flight during rioting in 1921 at the corner of York Street and Donegall Street, now the site of Belfast College of Art.

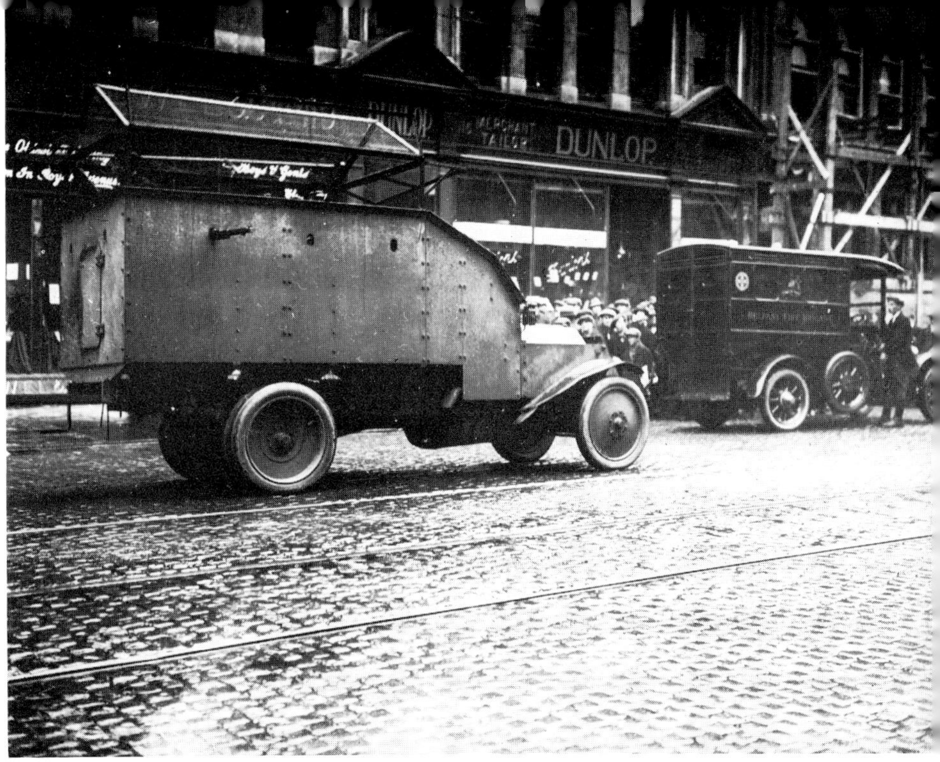

Above right: A Lancia armoured car used by police in Royal Avenue, Belfast, in 1922.

Right: Members of a "C" Specials patrol on duty in Albertbridge Road, Belfast, in 1922. The Special Constabulary was raised by the Westminster Government under the Special Constables (Ireland) Act of 1832 and there were three classes in which enlistment could be made —"A", "B" and "C".

Below: "A" Specials during an exercise in the Clogher Valley in 1922.

Above: A military post in York Street, one of the 1922 trouble spots.

Below: Mullagh Bridge, damaged by a bomb during the terrorist campaign of 1922.

Below: Ballagh Bridge, Co. Fermanagh, destroyed by terrorists in April 1922.

Above: Members of a "B" Specials unit in the Twenties.

elow: Members of the "B" Special Constabulary at a road block ear Ballycastle, Co. Antrim, in 1932.

Below: The shored-up battered doorway of Lisnaskea Police Barracks, target of a terrorist attack in 1956.

Below left: The Customs Post at Strabane, Co. Tyrone, after a bomb explosion in 1957.

Above: Creggan Bridge on the Newry Crossmaglen Road after a terrorist bomb explosion in 1957.

Above: Havoc after a terrorist bomb blast on the main Belfast/Dublin railway line near Goraghwood in 1957.

Below: Wreckage caused by a bomb placed on the Belfast/Dublin railway line at Kilnasaggart Bridge in 1961.

Below: A wrecked Ulster Transport Authority bus after attack in 1961.

Left: The scene as Civil Rights marchers reached Craigavon Bridge, Londonderry, in November, 1968.

Left: Confrontation at Burntollet Bridge, Co. Londonderry, in January, 1969.

Below: Police at a burning barricade across Shankill Road, Belfast, which was littered with stones and debris following a riot outbreak in 1968.

Above left: Troops behind barbed wire barriers at the junction of Coates Street and Sackville Place, Belfast, during the city's 1968 disturbances.

Left: Barricade on the outskirts of Belfast.

Below: Members of one of the peace committees of all denominations formed in Belfast during the height of the disturbances.

Above: During one of the 1968 street clashes a petrol bomb is seen exploding beneath a police armoured car in Divis Street, Belfast.

Above right: Conway Street, which leads directly from the Falls Road to Shankill Road, suffered badly during the Belfast disturbances of 1968.

Right: Barricade at Short Strand, Belfast, 1969.

Below: Sir Arthur Young, Chief Constable, inspecting recruits at the R.U.C. training centre in Enniskillen.

War

Pages Eighty to Ninety-One

Above: HMS Belfast, the cruiser built by Harland & Wolff in Belfast just before the Second World War. The ship took part in the fleet operations which led to the sinking of the battle cruiser Scharnhorst off the North Cape on 26 December 1943. The Belfast is believed to have fired the first shot of the heavy naval bombardment which preceded the Allied landing in Normandy.

Below: P38 bombers en route from dock to base through the empty early-morning streets of war-time Belfast.

Below: Members of the 2nd Battalion the Royal Ulster Rifles at Dunkirk.

Above: In common with other areas the Newtownards Road suffered heavily in the bombing of Belfast by German planes in 1941.

Above: Some of the children evacuated from Belfast after the first air-raid in 1941.

Below: The scene in High Street, Belfast, on the morning after a "fire raid" by German bombers.

Above: The wrecked Belfast Corporation tramcar depot in Salisbury Avenue, Antrim Road, after one of the German bombing raids.

Above: The Senate Chamber in the Parliament Buildings in use as an Operations Room by the Royal Air Force during the war.

Below: Soldiers and workers enjoy music from a small organ which escaped destruction in a blitzed Belfast Church Hall.

Above: Navigational aids used by the German Luftwaffe included these maps of Ballykelly and St. Angelo airfields.

Below: First American soldier to land in Northern Ireland on January 26, 1942, Private First Class Milburn Henke.

Below: Men of the United States Army's 34th Infantry Division have a snack after disembarking at Belfast. This was the first landing of US Forces in Europe in World War II.

Above: The Belfast built Short Sunderland flying boat, which played a big role in the war against U-boats.

Centre: Belfast girl munition workers visit a Royal Artillery site.

Below: Warships at anchor in Bangor Bay prior to the Normandy landing.

Above: Air landing by the 1st Battalion the Royal Ulster Rifles in the Rhine area in 1945.

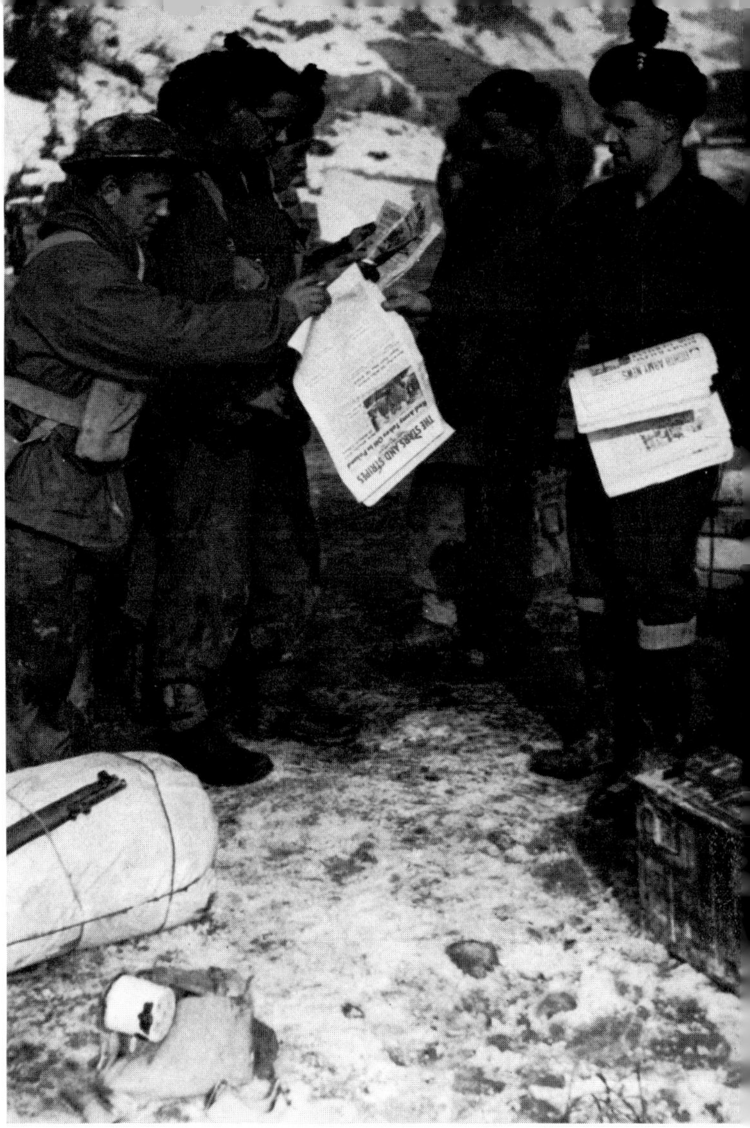

Above: Copies of 8th Army News reach men of the Royal Irish Fusiliers at St. Clemente during the Italian campaign.

Above: Men of the Royal Inniskilling Fusiliers landing near Algiers during the 500-ship convoy invasion of North Africa.

Above: Colonel Robert Blair Mayne, leader of the Special Air Service in World War II, who destroyed more enemy aircraft with his own hands and won more decorations than any other Serviceman. He became a legend in his own lifetime for his raids behind enemy lines. In one day he personally destroyed 47 enemy aircraft. He was awarded four DSOs and the French Legion of Honour.

Right: Londonderry, which played a major part in the critical anti-submarine battle, received the surrender of clutches of German U-boats at the close of hostilities. Here they are pictured at Lisahally.

Above: Leading Seaman James Magennis of Belfast—who won the Victoria Cross in a successful midget submarine attack on the Japanese cruiser Takao—is honoured by his native city. The submarine's commander, Lieutenant Ian E. Fraser, was also awarded the V.C. He manoeuvred it under the keel of Takao and Magennis attached six limpet mines to the cruiser's hull. For forty-five minutes he worked, scraping away the barnacles, and attaching the mines in pairs. Though handicapped by a steady leakage of oxygen, he completed the job before returning, exhausted, to the craft.

Right: The carrier HMS Eagle leaves Belfast shipyard in October 1951 for commissioning. Eagle was launched by the Princess Elizabeth (later Queen Elizabeth II) in 1946.

Left: Men of the North Irish Horse pictured during the victory parade in Tunis in 1943, and *centre*: recovering a Churchill tank during the campaign in Italy.

Left: A tank of the King's Royal Irish Hussars crossing the canal at Dongen on 30 October, 1944.

Left: A patrol of the Royal Inniskilling Fusiliers led by Sergeant Trainor of Whiteabbey in action in the Anzio Bridgehead during the Italian campaign. Sergeant Trainor won the Military Medal during the battle of the Sangro River.

Left: Hamburg and the end of 3,000 miles of fighting—4 May, 1945. The Hussars crossing the Kiel Canal.

Left: Supplies on mule-back for the Royal Irish Fusiliers Brigade H.Q. during the Italian campaign.

Construction

Pages Ninety-Two to One Hundred & One

Above: Belfast's City Hall, an impressive Portland stone building in Renaissance style.

Above: Multi-storey flats near Dunmurry, Co. Antrim, built by the Northern Ireland Housing Trust.

Below: Northern Ireland's Royal Courts of Justice in which sits the Supreme Court of Judicature. The building was opened in 1933.

Above: Dundonald House which accommodates the staff of three Northern Ireland Ministries. It was opened in 1963 and the main building has 12 storeys.

Below: The 11-storey North West Hospital at Altnagelvin, near Londonderry. It was built in 1960 and was the first large general and maternity unit constructed in the United Kingdom after World War II ended in 1945. It stands on a 50 acre site and has accommodation for more than 400 patients.

Below: One of several new hotels—the Europa in Great Victoria Street—being built in Belfast.

Above: Transport House, Belfast, headquarters of the Amalgamated Transport and General Workers Union.

Left: The M1, which extends thirty-eight miles from Belfast to Dungannon.

Below left: Another view of the M1 motorway.

Above: *From left to right*: Mr. W. J. Blease, Secretary of the Northern Ireland Committee of the Irish Congress of Trade Unions; the Minister of Health and Social Services (the Rt. Hon. W. K. Fitzsimmons); Mr. Victor Feather, General Secretary of the Trade Union Congress; and Mr. R. Roberts, General Secretary of the Irish Congress of Trade Unions.

Below: The Queen Elizabeth Bridge over the River Lagan in Belfast, opened in 1966. On the right is Queen's Bridge, opened in 1843.

Below: Part of the intersection linking the Sydenham by-pass with Belfast.

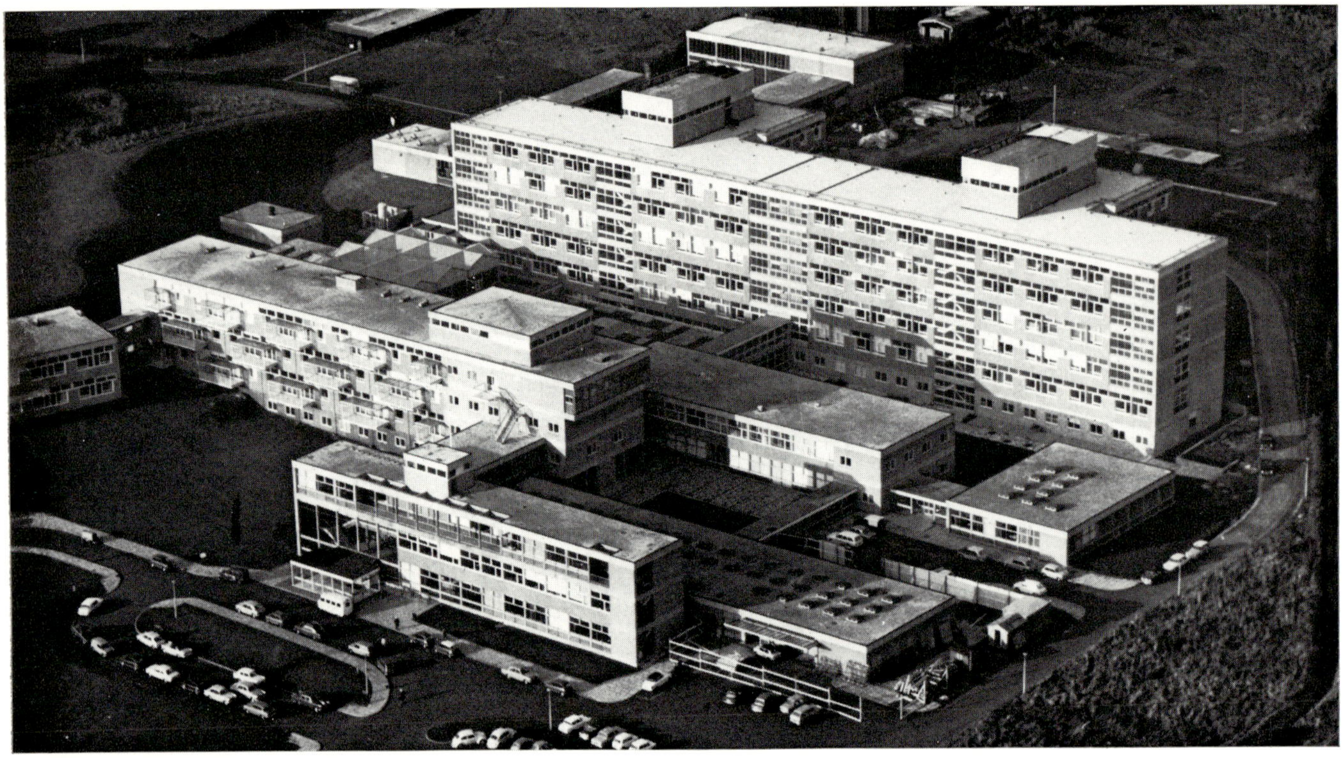

Above: Development of the Northern Ireland hospital services included the construction of six new hospitals between the end of World War II and the beginning of the 1970s. One is the Ulster Hospital, Dundonald, near Belfast, which has 550 beds.

Left: Another of the new hospitals, Musgrave Park Hospital, Belfast. This is a south view of the Nurses' Home complex with the School of Nursing on the left and the eight-floor Nurses' Home and recreation hall on the right.

Above: A striking air view of the M2 motorway near Ballymena, Co. Antrim.

Right: The modern style extension to the Ulster Museum in Belfast which has been ingeniously married to the original building of traditional Portland stone.

Right: Passengers boarding a jet flight to London at Aldergrove Airport. Passenger traffic—now more than 1,000,000 —is expected to pass the $1\frac{1}{2}$ million mark in 1975. More than £3 million is to be spent on extending the main runway and improving the terminal building.

Above: An artist's conception of part of the proposed Belfast ring road, one of the most imaginative overhead urban motorways planned for a British city.

Right: Craigavon housing development.

Below: Strathfoyle housing estate on the outskirts of Londonderry.

Above: Housing in Craigavon, Co. Armagh.

Below: Multi-storey flats in Bogside, Londonderry.

Industry and Agriculture

Pages One Hundred & Two to One Hundred & Fifteen

Above: The aircraft carrier, Bulwark, is launched at Belfast shipyard in 1948.

Left: William Ritchie, Belfast shipbuilding pioneer, who helped to make Ulster's name famous by building ships for the world.

Below: The late Sir Frederick Rebbeck (left) 'Mr. Shipbuilding', who handled the destinies of Harland & Wolff for more than 30 years up to 1962. He died in 1964. With Sir Frederick are (centre) Mr. Macmillan and Lord Brookeborough.

Above: The 45,000-ton liner, Canberra, one of the biggest passenger ships to be built in a British yard in the post-war years. The Canberra was launched at Belfast in 1960.

Right: The oil tanker, Myrina, after its launch by Harland & Wolff at Belfast in 1967. It was the largest vessel built in Europe up to that time—192,250 tons and 1,050 feet long.

Below: A typical group of Belfast shipyardmen. Size of the Queen's Island labour force is in the region of 10,000.

Above: A Seacat anti-aircraft missile built at Short Bros. and Harland's, Belfast, and installed on board Derwent, the Australian Navy's guided weapon destroyer.

Above left: The super-tanker Esso Ulidia (253,000 tons) under construction in the world's biggest building dock at Queen's Island Belfast. The world's largest crane puts in place a 500-ton section of her upper decks. The crane has a height of 316 feet, a span of 460 feet and can lift up to 840 tons.

Left: The dry dock at East Twin, 1,100 feet long and 165 feet wide at the entrance, is one of the world's largest. In the dock is the Shell tanker, Mangelia (206,000 tons), overhauled by Harland & Wolff in 1970.

Above: The SC1 VTOL experimental aircraft designed and built by Short Bros. and Harland as part of the Ministry of Aviation's research programme.

The Short Skyvan, a small and adaptable aircraft used chiefly for freight, and one of the top products of the Belfast aircraft factory at Short Bros. and Harland.

A Short Belfast strategic freighter built for the R.A.F. at Belfast aircraft factory.

The Skyliner, another Belfast aircraft factory product is a passenger version of Skyvan.

The end product of Northern Ireland's great linen industry—Irish linen damask in traditional oak leaf design which shows fine silver, glass and china to advantage.

Northern Ireland's linen industry employs some 28,000 men and women. Shown in operation is a Jacquard loom for weaving linen damask.

An inspector testing multiples of a group selector rack at the Standard Telephone and Cables factory at Monkstown.

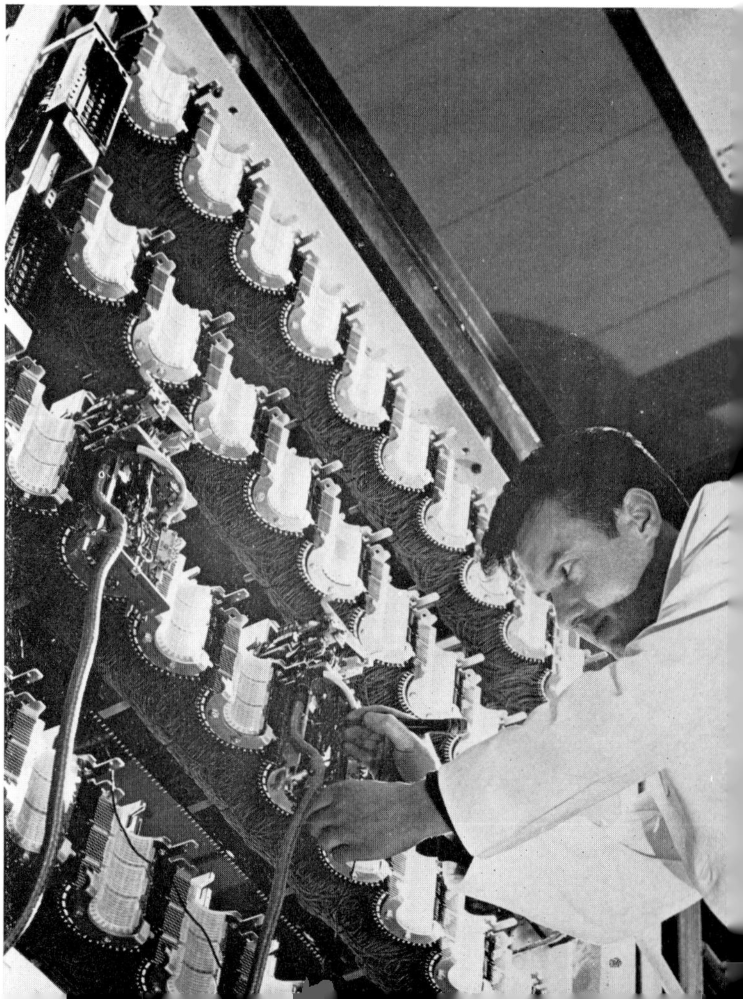

Above: A study in concentration at the engineering components factory in Londonderry of Molins Ltd.

Above: A panel is checked on an electronic calculator at the works at Castlereagh, Belfast, of International Computers and Tabulators.

Above: The new industries programme of the Ministry of Commerce has succeeded in attracting some of the world's biggest manufacturing organisations to Northern Ireland—among them, Monsanto of the United States.

Below: The British Enkalon factory near Antrim.

Above left: Du Pont plant at Maydown, Londonderry, one of the thirty-plus American plants in Northern Ireland.

Above: Coolkeeragh Power Station, Maydown.

Centre left: Carreras tobacco factory at Carrickfergus, Co. Antrim.

Below left: Gas for the city as well as oil for the country is produced in this refinery on the shores of Belfast Lough.

Below: Goodyear is making an important contribution to the prosperity of the new city of Craigavon.

Above: Livestock husbandry is the basis of Northern Ireland's agriculture.

Below: Milk sold by Northern Ireland's 15,000 licensed milk producers exceeds 156 million gallons a year. The largest quantity of milk manufactured is used for butter-making and in this picture 1-lb rolls are mechanically packed in tinfoil wrappers.

Below: Milk is bottled at a Northern Ireland dairy centre. More than 44 million gallons are sold as liquid milk every year.

Above: Agriculture is Northern Ireland's biggest single industry and here are seen sheep on an Ulster farm.

Below: Yoghurt is another important Northern Ireland dairy product and it is shown being mechanically packed.

Below: Veterinary research has developed into one of the most important branches of the Northern Ireland Ministry of Agriculture. In one of the research laboratories a technical officer uses an electron microscope to examine viruses at a magnification of 100,000.

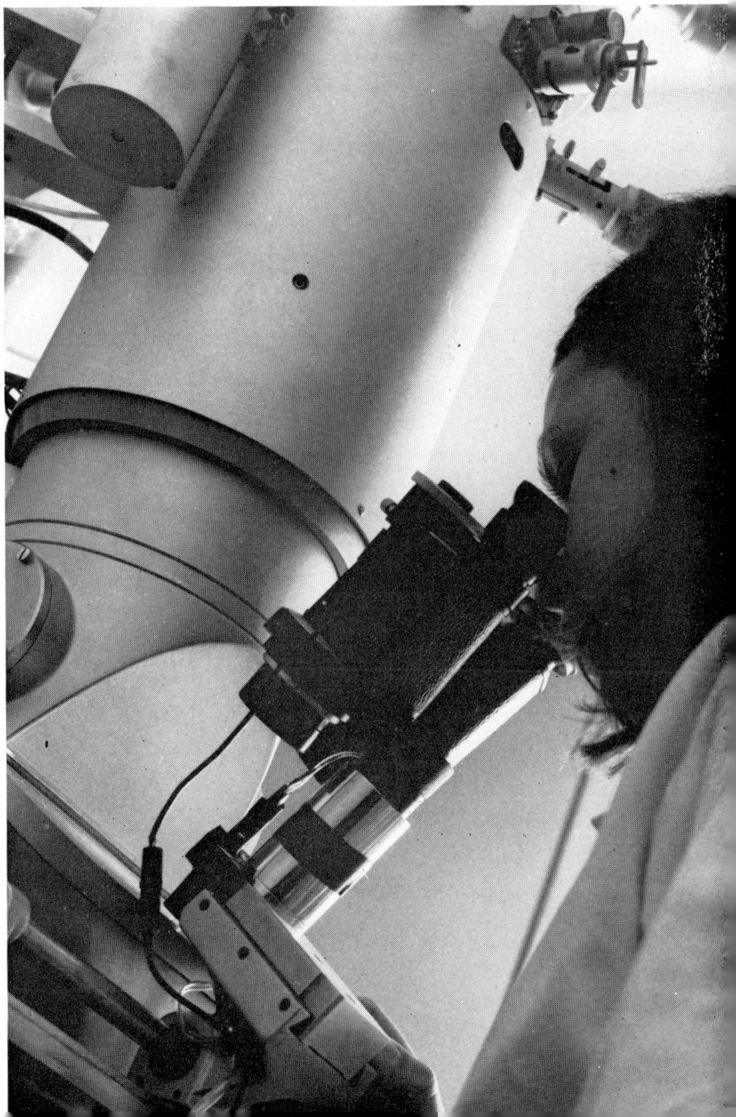

Above: The Northern Ireland poultry industry has an annual output worth about £22½ million or 18 per cent of the total agricultural output. Our picture illustrates feeding in battery cages.

Above: More than 100,000 acres of trees have been planted in Northern Ireland in the post-war years.

Below: An increasingly modern and well-equipped sea-fishing fleet is increasing the value of its landings. This is Ardglass, an important herring fishing centre.

Above: A substantial proportion of all the new roses in Britain are produced in Northern Ireland by two firms, McGredys and Dicksons. Above is Sam McGredy and his wife. He is reputed to be the second largest rose breeder in the world and has 350 acres of nurseries.

Right: Alex Dickson, 77, of Newtownards and his son Patrick, famous for their roses. The firm has won every major rose-growing award.

Left: On a Northern Ireland farm a double crop forage harvester fills into a trailer alongside. Northern Ireland farms are highly mechanised.

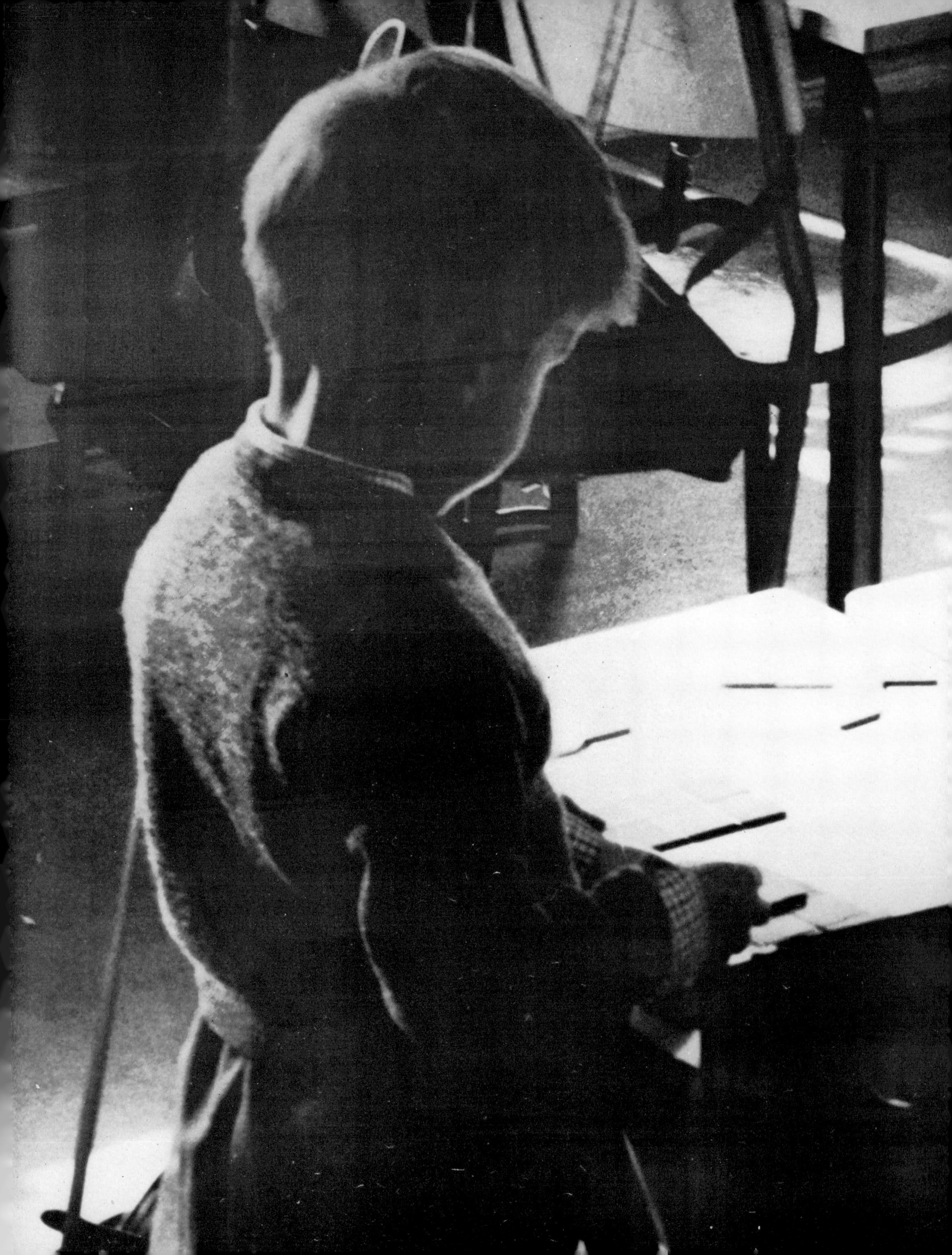

Education

Pages One Hundred & Sixteen to One Hundred & Twenty-Five

Above: Children in Ulster usually start school when they are five years old but many nursery schools, like this one in New Lodge Road, Belfast, are in operation for children aged two to five.

Left: Primary school at Derrygonnelly, Co. Fermanagh.

Right: The school orchestra of Cross and Passion College, Ballycastle, Co. Antrim.

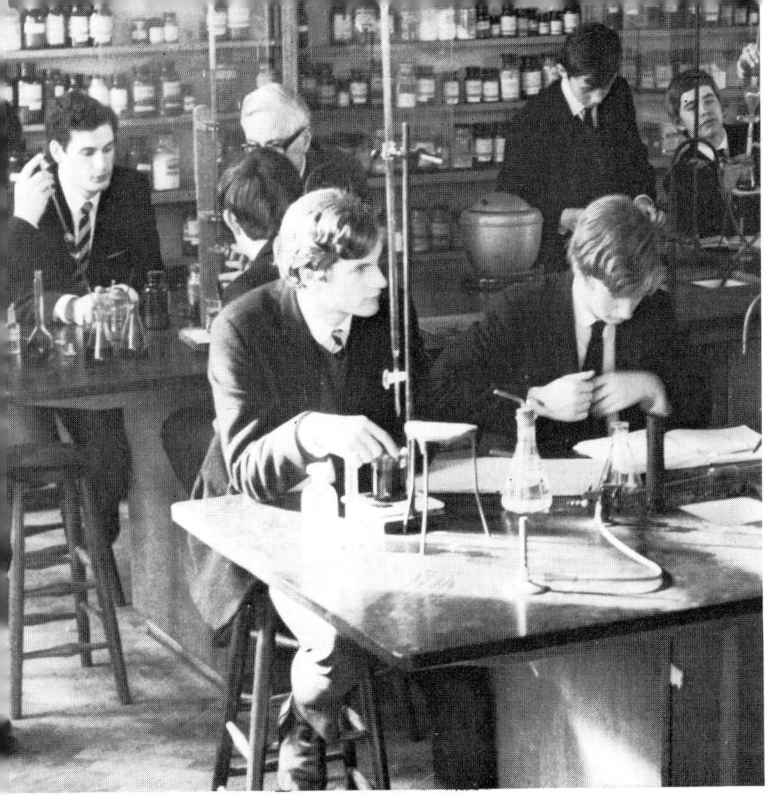

In the chemistry laboratory of Campbell College, Belfast, one of Northern Ireland's best known grammar schools.

Pottery is taught in the art department of St. Joseph's Secondary School, Londonderry.

Above left: Junior pupils in the well-equipped gymnasium of Fivemiletown High School, Co. Tyrone.

Centre left: The Ulster College of Physical Education at Newtownabbey, Co. Antrim. Here pupils demonstrate a modern educational dance.

Above right: The language laboratory at Stranmillis teacher training college.

Below left: The up-to-date theatre at Stranmillis.

Right: Approving the hemline at the College of Domestic Science, Belfast.

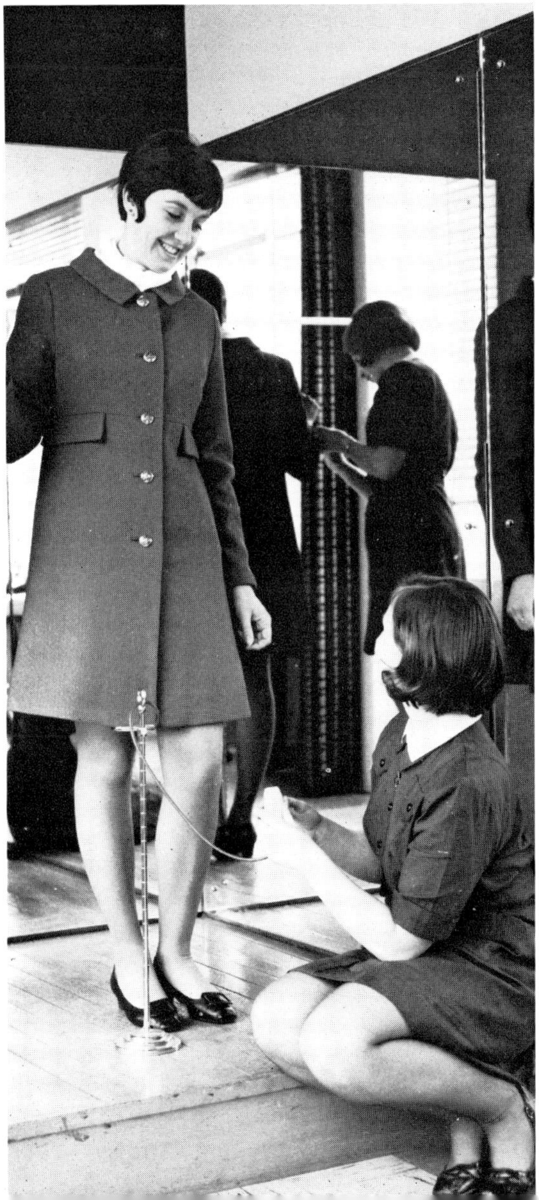

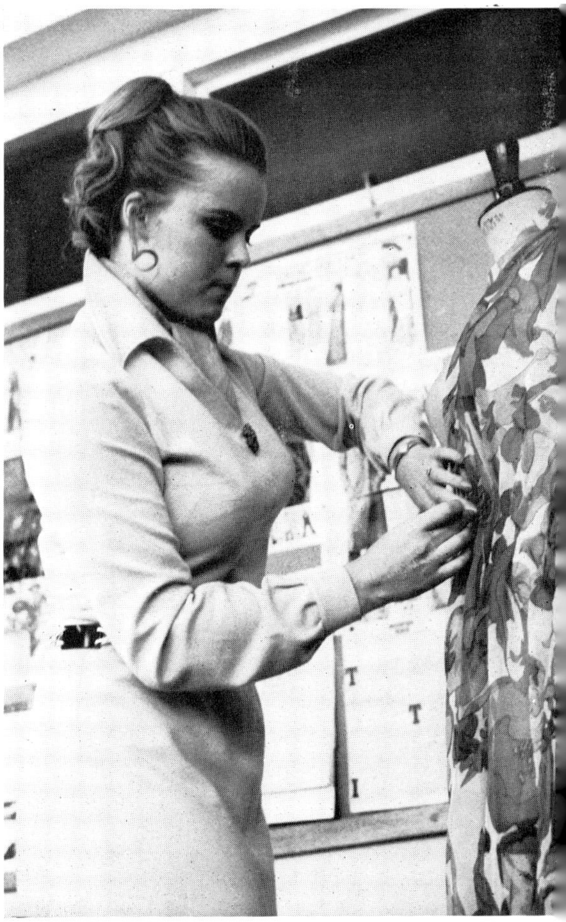

Above: A student working in the textile and fashion department of the Ulster College of Art and Design.

Below: The Queen's University of Belfast, which has close on 7,000 students.

Above: The Ulster College of Art and Design.

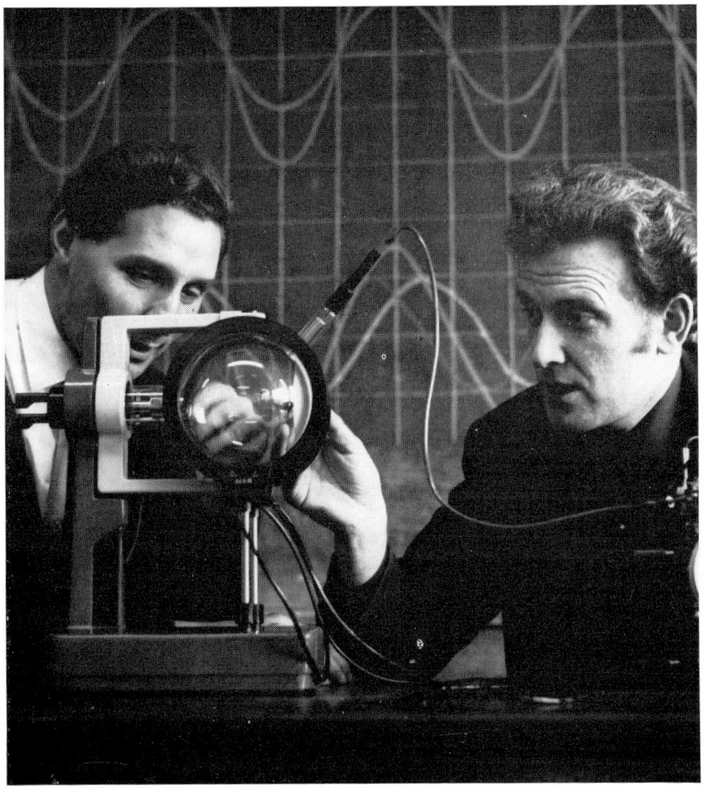

Institutions of further education provide instruction in commercial, scientific, technological and domestic subjects for persons over compulsory school age. Here techniques are demonstrated at Ballymena Technical College.

Northern Ireland's industrial training programme is one of the most advanced in Europe. Apprentices in an instrumentation and control class test an electronic appliance at one of eight Government Training Centres.

Below: The New University of Ulster at Coleraine. It is anticipated that it will have 2,200 full-time students by 1973.

Larne Technical College. The Social Science Building at Queen's.

Right: Students working in the Physics Laboratory at St. Joseph's Teacher Training College.

The modern Science and Engineering Building of the Queen's University.

The Arts

Pages One Hundred & Twenty-Six to One Hundred & Thirty-Five

Above: William Conor, famous for hi
paintings of the local scene and the peopl

Left: Sir John Lavery, distinguished Belfast-born painter, 1856–1941.

Right: Sir Hamilton Harty, con
poser, one of Ulster's mo
distinguished sons in the cultur
field.

Above: Robert Lynd, author and journalist. When he died in 1949 he was Britain's leading essayist.

Above: St John Ervine, author and playwright, 1883–1971. Wrote Ulster's longest running play, Boyd's Shop, and many others which had successful runs in London. For many years "Observer" theatre critic.

Below: Forrest Reid, distinguished Ulster novelist.

Above left: Louis MacNeice, Ulster-born poet and radio dramatist, 1907–1963.

Others on this page are Ulster personalities who have made their mark on stage and screen: J. G. Devlin, Stephen Boyd and Richard Todd are pictured above.

On the left is Joe Tomelty and on the right Elizabeth Begley and Harold Goldblatt.

Above: Colin Blakeley, Belfast actor, star of many film and TV productions.

Left: James Young, Belfast actor—famous for his portrayals of the Belfast character and the Ulster dialect.

Below: James Ellis, Belfast actor, member of the TV 'Z Car' team.

Above and right: Two of a number of contemporary Ulster artists who have established themselves in the front rank—Colin Middleton and T. P. Flanagan.

Below: Greer Garson, Hollywood actress, born in Larne, Co. Antrim.

Left: Michael Emmerson, organiser of several successful Queen's University Festivals of Art.

Above: The history and industries of Belfast are represented in this mural by John Luke, painted as part of the city's contribution to the 1951 Festival of Britain. It is on the first floor of Belfast City Hall.

Left: Patricia Mulholland's Irish ballet is world famous. The legends, songs and stories of the country have been transformed into enchanting folk dances which are completely her own. An accomplished violinist and choreographer, Miss Mulholland is pictured playing her music for "Children of Lir".

Left: Ulster dancing by members of the First Lisburn Girls' Brigade, wearing costumes of Ulster tartan and of millworkers of the last century.

Right: One of the best-known and most controversial works of Ulster born sculptor, F. E. McWilliam, is Princess Macha, which stands at the entrance of Altnagelvin Hospital, Londonderry.

Below: The Ulster Orchestra, formed in 1966, and the first fully professional Northern Ireland Orchestra.

DUNLOP

Sport

Pages One Hundred & Thirty-Six to One Hundred & Forty-Five

Above: The 1929 Ulster Tourist Trophy car race in progress on the old Ards Circuit. The view is from Quarry Corner. The race was staged on the Ards Circuit 1928–1936 and on the Dundrod Circuit 1950–1955.

Below: World flyweight boxing champion Rinty Monaghan (centre) pictured with Jackie Patterson after he had beaten the Scot in the King's Hall, Balmoral, Belfast.

Below: Trigo, Derby winner in 1929, was owned by the Barnett family of Belfast.

Above: C. R. Whitcroft, the 1932 winner with Mr. Ramsay MacDonald and Lord Craigavon.

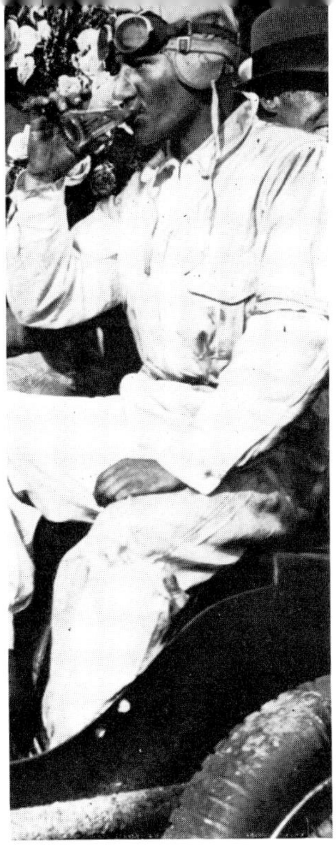

Above: Nuvolari, one of the great racing drivers of history, pictured after winning the 1933 race over the Ards circuit.

Above: The Duke of Edinburgh chats with Artie Bell before the start of the 1949 Senior T.T. in the Isle of Man, which Artie won the previous year. In the centre of the picture is another well-known motor-cycling racing figure, Ulster-born Joe Craig, Norton technical adviser and team manager.

Above: Air Vice-Marshal George Beamish, one of the all-time great rugby forwards. He graduated to international rugby via Coleraine Academical Institution.

Above: Fred Daly, Portrush-born golfer, who won both the British Open and Match play championships in 1947 and went on to win the match play title three times.

Above: Peter Doherty, Irish International inside-forward and manager of Northern Ireland's 1958 World Cup soccer team.

Above: Jimmy Warnock of Belfast who many considered was unlucky not to win a world title. He defeated the world champion twice but in non-title contests on each occasion.

Above: An early photograph of Joe Bambrick, idol of Linfield, Chelsea and Ireland. Joe scored a record-breaking six goals for Ireland against Wales at Windsor Park.

Above: Irish international soccer star Elisha Scott of Liverpool and Belfast Celtic—one of the greatest goalkeepers of all time.

Below: The great Belfast Celtic soccer team of 1949 on the eve of departure for an American tour, in the course of which they defeated a Scottish international touring side.

bove: Northern Ireland's soccer team covered itself with glory in the 1958 World up soccer finals in Sweden. Pictures show Danny Blanchflower (captain) leading the am into action, followed by Wilbur Cush, and (*right*) greeted by the then Governor Northern Ireland (Lord Wakehurst) before the start of the Northern Ireland/West ermany tie—one of the classics of the tournament which ended in a draw. The orthern Ireland players from left are: Jimmy McIlroy, Harry Gregg, Willie unningham and Danny Blanchflower.

Above: Freddie Gilroy, British and European boxing title-holder.

Below: Jack Kyle and Michael Gibson, both Irish internationals and both British Lions, and amongst the greatest rugby players in Irish history. Jack Kyle represented his country 46 times.

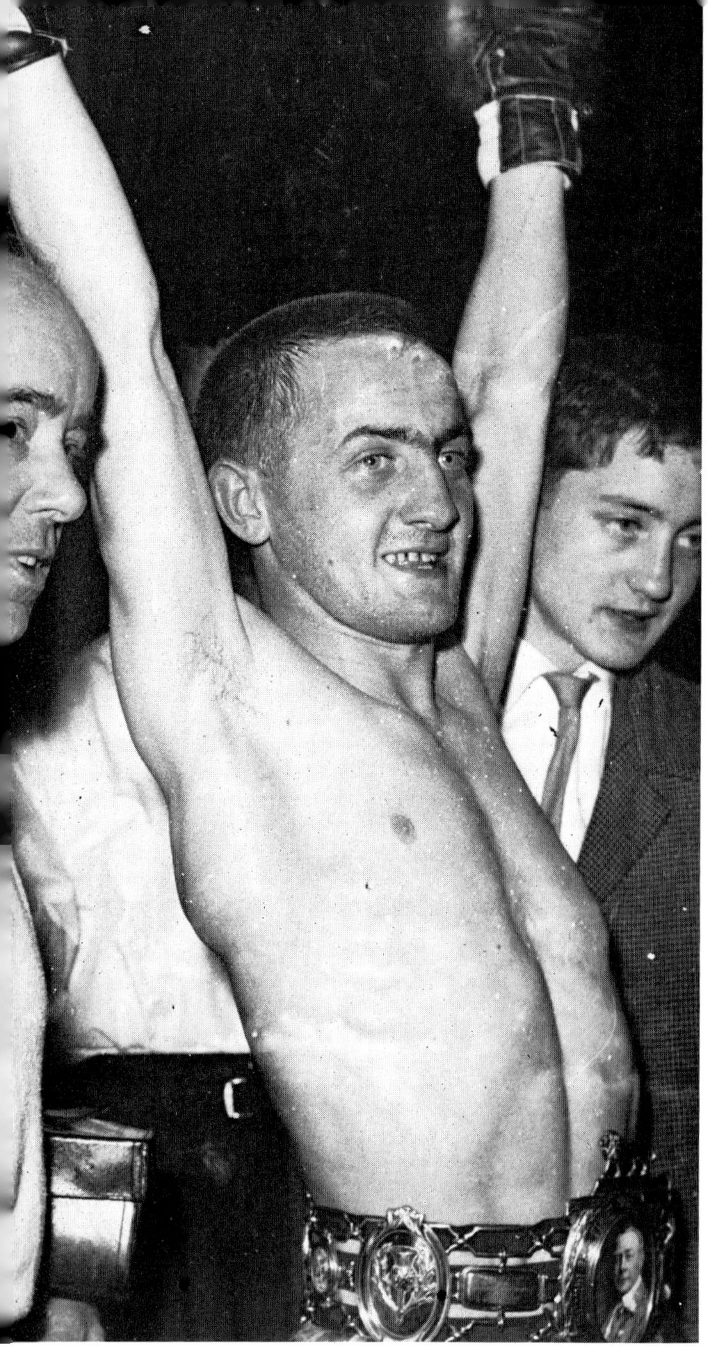

Above: Jim McCourt, Commonwealth Games Gold Medal winner and one of the greatest Ulster amateur boxers of all time.

Left: John Caldwell, who won the world bantamweight boxing championship in 1961 by defeating Alphonse Halimi of France.

Below: Ulster-born Robin Dixon and Englishman Tony Nash winning the two-man bobsleigh championship in the 1964 Olympic Games. Robin is the son of the Speaker of the Northern Ireland Senate (Lt. Col. The Rt. Hon. The Lord Glentoran).

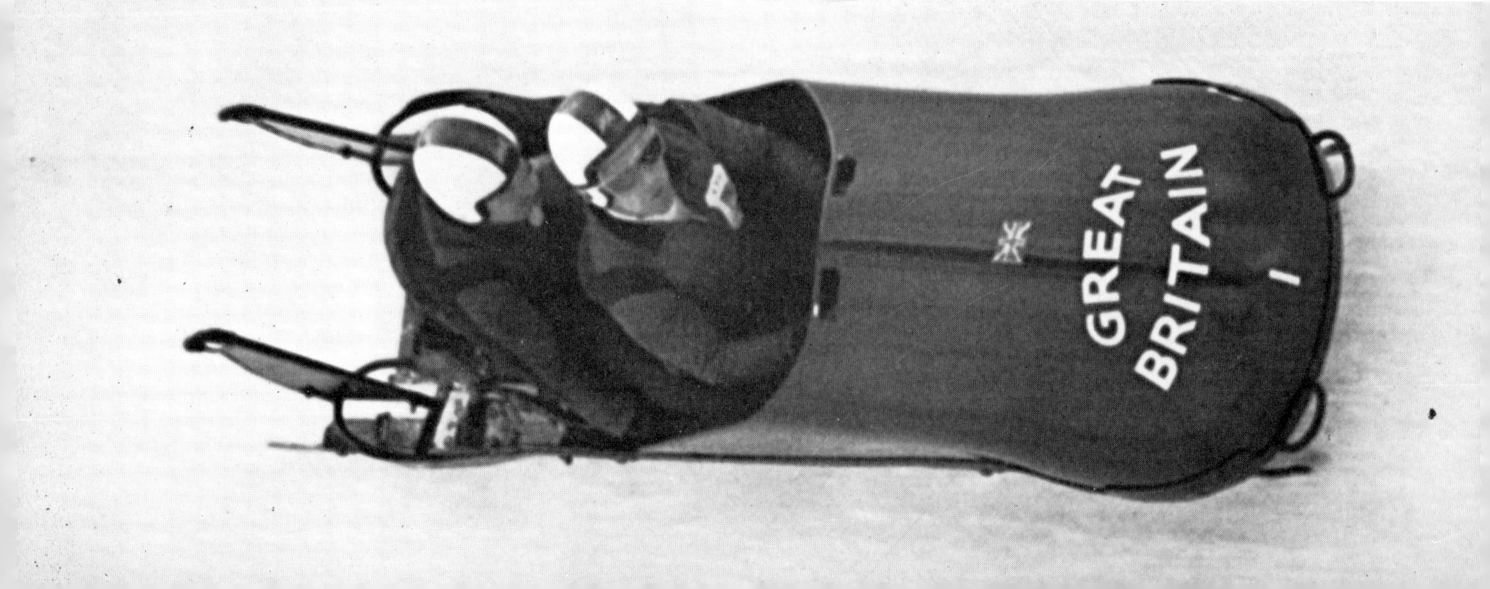

Above: The 1966 and 1968 winners of the Aintree Grand National—Anglo and Red Alligator—were both born and bred on the farm of Mr. William Kennedy at Dunanelly Inch, near Downpatrick. The horses were half-brothers, born of the same dam, Miss Alligator, who cost Mr. Kennedy seventy guineas.

Below: Paddy Hopkirk of Belfast, winner of the Monte Carlo Rally and of a host of other world-class events. He took second place in the London–Sydney marathon.

Above: Recent picture of the Ulster Grand Prix at Dundrod, one of the world championship motor cycle races.

Above: Down's brilliant gaelic football team, which defeated Kerry in the All-Ireland final, is received at the City Hall, Belfast.

Above: Joe Lennon, captain, thanks thousands of supporters who waited in the rain to welcome the team home.

Below: The Q.U.B.–Seeley 500 cc motor-cycle which was developed at the Queen's University, Belfast, by a team from the Faculty of Mechanical Engineering headed by Dr. Gordon Blair. All the design work on the engine was done by a computer.

Left: Belfast-born George Best of Manchester United, regarded by many as one of the three greatest soccer players alive today. Only Pele of Brazil and Eusabio of Portugal are considered to match him in genius.

Above: Mary Peters, Belfast secretary, who won a pentathlon gold medal at the Edinburgh Commonwealth Games, talking to the Prince of Wales, who handed over the awards. It was her second gold medal at the Games.

Above: Michael Bull of Belfast winning the pole-vault gold medal at the Edinburgh Commonwealth Games.

Below: Bowler extraordinary Roy Fulton of Coleraine (*right*) who has won many Irish and British singles and doubles titles. He is pictured here with doubles partner Charles Taylor.

Below: The Crossle car, which is in great demand on the racetracks of the world, and its designer, John Crossle of Holywood, Co. Down.

Scenic

Pages One Hundred & Forty-Six to One Hundred & Fifty-Seven

Above: The picturesque Glenelly Valley, Co. Tyrone.

Left: Trassey Bridge in the Mourne country of Co. Down.

Right: Tollymore Forest Park near Newcastle, one of many in the Province open to the public.

Right: Scrabo Tower dominates the peaceful Down countryside.

Above left: The White Rocks, Portrush, washed by the Atlantic.

Left: The Glens of Antrim, famous for their beauty.

Below: The bird sanctuary on the steep cliffs of Rathlin Island.

Above: The Giant's Causeway, often called the Eighth Wonder of the World.

Below: The 12th Century Norman Castle at Carrickfergus.

Left: The rivers of Ul
offer unlimited facilitie
for the angler.

Below left: Lough Er
heart of Ulster's beaut
ful lake district.

Above: The Mourne valley, Co. Tyrone.

Below: Dunluce Castle on the rugged North Antrim coast.

Below: The road to the Glens of Antrim.

bove left: Lough Neagh, biggest inland 'aterway in the British Isles.

'*elow left*: Royal Portrush golf links, set mid the wild grandeur of North Antrim.

Above: The Ulster Folk Museum at Cultra, visited every year by thousands of tourists.

Below: Golf at Cushendall in the shadows of majestic Lurigethan. Ulster has nearly 60 golf courses.

Below: The harbour and promenade, Portstewart, Co. Londonderry.

Above: Aerial view of Portora Royal School and the surrounding area of Lough Erne.

Below: Londonderry and the Craigavon Bridge pictured from the Waterside.

Above: Armagh has long been regarded as the ecclesiastical capital of Ireland. Pictured here are the St. Patrick's Church of Ireland Cathedral and the Roman Catholic Cathedral.

Below: Brooke Park, Londonderry.

Below: Apple blossom time in Co. Armagh, often described as the orchard of Ulster.

Transport, Tradition, Ulster American Links, and Gracious Homes

Pages One Hundred & Fifty-Eight to One Hundred & Sixty-Seven

EVOLUTION OF TRANSPORT

Right: The Portrush-Giant's Causeway Tramway Service, the first hydro-electric tramway in the world. The tram, driven by Miss Jeannie Richardson, Portrush, made its inaugural run in 1883. The order for its discontinuance and abandonment was dated November 1949.

On the left: Three typical examples of Ulster service buses and charabancs of the early twenties.

Right: A once-familiar sight was trains of the Clogher Valley railway running through Main Street, Fivemiletown. The railway was closed in the early 1940's.

Below: The Lough Neagh Queen, popular for pleasure cruises on Britain's biggest inland waterway.

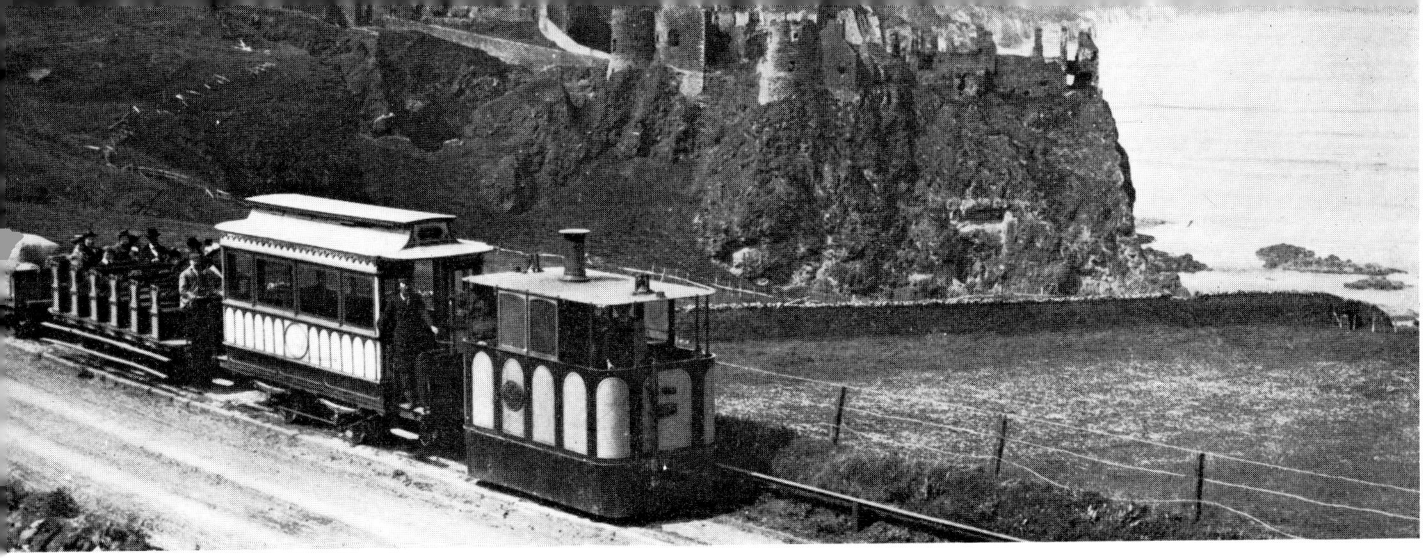

A modern 41-seater vehicle of Ulsterbus.

A modern diesel train operated by Northern Ireland Railways.

Steam trains ceased to run in 1970.

The pictures illustrate traditional parades of the Orange Order (above) and the Ancient Order of Hibernians (right).

The Orange parade takes place on July 12th and that of the A.O.H. on August 15th.

ULSTER AMERICAN LINKS

Below: Gray's printing house in Strabane, Co. Tyrone, in which John Dunlap served his apprenticeship before he went to the United States, where he printed the Declaration of Independence for the Congress in 1776, and in 1784 founded the Pennsylvania Packet, the first American daily newspaper. The premises are now in the care of the National Trust.

Above: The home at Dergalt, near Strabane, Co. Tyrone, in which the grandfather of Woodrow Wilson, 27th President of the United States of America (1913-1921) lived before he emigrated. The Northern Ireland Government bought the house and also the house at Cullybackey, Co. Antrim, in which the father of Chester Alan Arthur (21st President, 1881-1885) lived before he left for the United States about 1816. Both houses have been restored and the Wilson house is in the care of the National Trust.

Above: Ten presidents of the United States had their origins in Ulster, including three pictured here, from the left—Andrew Jackson (1829—1837), Ulysses S. Grant (1869—1877) and Woodrow Wilson (1913—1921).

Below: The cottage at Mountjoy, near Omagh, Co. Tyrone, which Thomas Mellon left in 1818 for America, where he founded one of the greatest financial institutions in the United States. The Mellon family established a trust fund for the restoration of the house, which has been taken over by the National Trust.

GRACIOUS HOUSES

Pictured here are some of the great houses in the care of the National Trust. These houses open every day except Tuesday during the season and are visited annually by hundreds of tourists.

Right: Springhill, Co. Londonderry.

Left: Florencecourt, Co. Fermanagh.

Left: Castleward, Co. Down..

Right: Ardress House, Co. Armagh.

Below: Castlecoole, Co. Fermanagh.

8. Administration—Reducing the Leeway

'Before there could be much initiating of new schemes, there was a great need to catch up on British standards in various departments of life.'

The powers of the government of Northern Ireland were restricted by the Government of Ireland Act, 1920, to internal matters; but the powers of a government depend not merely upon statutes but also very much upon money. The old Dublin administration, prior to the coming into operation of the 1920 Act, had been financed by the United Kingdom Exchequer, into which the taxation revenue of Ireland as a whole had been paid. In 1897 the Childers Commission had reported that, by the method by which revenue was allocated to Ireland, Ireland had for many years been heavily over-taxed in relation to its resources.

Those who devised the Act of 1920 did not entirely escape from the attraction of the methods which had been employed in the past. The Act directed that, in effect, the taxation revenue of Ireland was to go into the United Kingdom Exchequer, that from it certain deductions should be made to meet Ireland's share of certain public expenditures and 'the Irish contribution towards Imperial liabilities and expenditure', and the rest should be divided between the two Irish governments by a joint exchequer board.

The withdrawal of the Irish Free State from the United Kingdom and its fiscal separation from the United Kingdom, which occurred on 1 April, 1923, left the financial position of Northern Ireland open to reconsideration and in need of adjustment. Representations to that effect were made by the Northern Ireland government to the Chancellor of the Exchequer, and a Special Arbitration Committee was established in January, 1923, to examine the position and report on it. Known as the Colwyn committee, it consisted of Lord Colwyn as chairman, Sir Laming Worthington-Evans and Sir Josiah Stamp, with Mr. William Piercy as secretary.

This committee reported in 1924 and 1925 on the complex case presented by the Northern Ireland government, giving decisive rulings upon a wide variety of financial questions arising from the winding up of the older system of Irish public finances and the necessary allocation or apportionment of various funds and liabilities between north and south and between Northern Ireland and the United Kingdom. It was a great tidying-up operation. Basically the recommendations of the Colwyn committee were a response to the case ably presented on behalf of the Northern Ireland government. The satisfactory outcome of the prolonged negotiations and the pattern of financial relationship which has continued to this day between the governments of the United Kingdom and of Northern Ireland may thus be attributed in large measure to the anonymous civil servants at the Northern Ireland Ministry of Finance who prepared the material submitted to the committee and in particular to the late Sir Ernest Clark, then permanent secretary to that Ministry.

Broadly speaking, the taxation of Northern Ireland has always been the same as that in all other parts of the United Kingdom and goes into the United Kingdom Exchequer. Against this sum deductions are made by the Treasury to meet certain pre-1920 liabilities of Northern Ireland. Then a sum is handed over to the Northern Ireland government to enable it to carry on the services for which it is responsible and meet the tasks which have been delegated to it.

The amount of this sum is decided by a joint exchequer board consisting of a representative each from the United Kingdom Treasury and the Northern Ireland Ministry of Finance, with a chairman appointed by the Crown. This board decides the amount to be handed over to the Northern Ireland government on the principle that Northern Ireland shall have parity with the rest of the United Kingdom in social services and equality in other matters, due regard being had to local circumstances.

Anything that is left over out of the taxation revenue which has gone from Northern Ireland into the United Kingdom Exchequer after this payment to the Northern Ireland government forms the 'Imperial contribution' and represents Northern Ireland's contribution to general United Kingdom expenditure, such as the armed forces and the diplomatic service. In this way the Imperial contribution is left an elastic factor instead of being a fixed amount or a fixed proportion of the revenue raised in Northern Ireland. The corresponding portion of the revenue remains self-adjusting in other parts of the United Kingdom by the automatic effect of the pooling of resources; but the same effect has to be brought about for Northern Ireland by the machinery of the joint exchequer board, since Northern Ireland's public finances, unlike those of other parts of the United Kingdom, are segregated from the full effects of pooling.

A very small range of excise duties and other taxation, imposed by the Northern Ireland government itself, has tended to be kept at the same level as similar taxes in Britain.

Although this method of allocating taxation revenue to Northern Ireland is strictly fair and has ensured that people there pay and receive no more and no less than people elsewhere in the United Kingdom, its complexity gave rise over the years to a good deal of misunderstanding. For example the payment to Northern Ireland appeared for many years in United Kingdom public accounts simply as an item of expenditure with nothing to indicate that there had been a corresponding intake of revenue from Northern Ireland, creating for some the impression that Northern Ireland was being given an enormous free gift every year at the expense of the British taxpayer.

The government of Northern Ireland had thus little freedom to manoeuvre financially. It could go step by step with Britain in any new development requiring government expenditure, but it could not go beyond this. It did, however, have great administrative freedom. It had to cut its coat to suit the size of the cloth provided; but it was quite free to exercise much ingenuity in the cutting. So long as it did not involve heavy additional expenditure, nearly any new approach could be taken to any government problem, or to any experiment in methods. An important feature of the later history of Northern Ireland was therefore to be a series of pioneering experiments in government intervention in the economy of the province.

Before there could be much initiating of new schemes, however, there was a great need to catch up on British standards in various departments of life. The first great need was a new education system. Since 1902 the present system of local education authorities administering various types of schools in their areas had been established in Britain; but Ireland had been exempted from the 1902 Education Act at the request of the Irish Nationalists at Westminster. It was felt that it would be a disturbing measure in Ireland where such a high proportion of the schools were administered by religious orders or were otherwise under Church control; and the British government did not wish to interfere in this field.

The government of Northern Ireland now resolved to make up lost ground in education and place the public education system on a level with that in Britain. A departmental committee on the educational services in Northern Ireland was established in September, 1921, under the chairmanship of Mr. R. J. Lynn, later Sir Robert Lynn. Although the committee was intended to represent the widest possible range of opinion in the province, Roman Catholics would not serve on it and rejected all invitations to present views or evidence to it. The committee expressed deep regret at this but stated in its interim report of 1922, 'We hope that notwithstanding the disadvantage at which we were placed by this action it will be found that Roman Catholic interests have not suffered. We have throughout been careful to keep in mind and to make allowance for the particular points of view of Roman Catholics in regard to education, so far as known to us, and it has been our desire to refrain as far as we could from recommending any course which might be thought to be contrary to their wishes.'

The final report of the Lynn Committee was presented in 1923 and an education bill based upon its recommendations was at once proceeded with. Local education authorities were to be formed by county councils and county borough councils, with power to appoint smaller regional committees. The foundation of a non-denominational state education system was thus laid. At the primary level the schools were described as public elementary schools. The Roman Catholic bishops issued a statement declaring that 'the proposed schools are impossible for our children'. There was provision, however, for the continued existence of a wide range of voluntary schools outside the non-denominational state system, and these received grants and salary payments as in the past. Public funds were made available on an increasingly generous scale for maintenance and building outlay on voluntary schools, until latterly there has been little to choose financially between the position of a voluntary school or one inside the state system. Protestant religious bodies also attacked the new education system because it did not make provision for religious instruction. Some religious instruction was therefore made permissive in 1925.

On the economic side there was government intervention to impose controls which might improve the standard and reputation of the province's products. A Marketing of Eggs Act was passed in 1924, the first of a long series of acts and regulations which gradually imposed increasingly high standards upon the quality and handling of agricultural products, guided and educated farmers, eliminated diseases of animals, improved livestock and developed research. Steady progress in these policies transformed what had been a very backward province in agriculture into the most progressive and productive agricultural area in the British Isles.

But in the 1920s, though the wisdom of hindsight can see that these first tentative government interventions to bring about improvement and reform in a variety of social and economic matters were to reveal a great and valuable potential, progress was yet very slow, and it was not until the 1930s that the first government efforts were made to transform the industrial life of the province. It was not easy to outpass certain 'free enterprise' inhibitions. Government intervention or the creation of anything that seemed like a monopoly caused much uneasiness. Government encourageemnt was given to a coalmining enterprise in Tyrone in 1924; and in 1928 Belfast Corporation was given a monopoly of public passenger transport in the city after a chaotic period of free competition. But the troubles of industry were still treated largely as if they were as incapable of modification as the weather. External trade, with which so many of these troubles were bound up, was the affair of Westminster and Whitehall and not of the Northern Ireland government. Yet the Northern Ireland government found itself increasingly held responsible by sections of the public for the high unemployment rate in the province.

By the middle 1920s the climate of the province's social and political life was indeed much calmer. The curfew order which had been used during the worst of the troubled times was finally revoked in 1924, and the next year a run-down of security forces began with the disbanding of the 3,500 'A' Specials. This caused an outcry. Indignantly the men barricaded themselves into their barracks, in some cases kidnapping their officers, and demanded a gratuity of £200 each. The government offered the alternative of a concession of two months' leave on full pay or dismissal in forty-eight hours, and the mutiny ended. The government still held some republican internees, and the cases of such political prisoners were now referred by the Northern Ireland government to the British cabinet for review.

A general election in 1925 brought a more healthy variety to parliament with the election of 32 Unionists, four independent Unionists, three Labour, one representative of tenants, ten Nationalists and two republicans. Under the leadership of the late Joseph Devlin, the Nationalists now took their seats in parliament and acted as an opposition instead of abstaining. Devlin was a powerful influence. His humane concern for the problems of the poorest people did much to rally to the support of his party the sympathies of working people and to unite to some extent the causes of nationalism and labour. His quick caustic tongue brought a new vitality into parliamentary debates; and, if a confident parliamentary majority had created any kind of happy daydream or euphoria in any members on the government side, Devlin quickly dissipated it. At the same time his great good humour was a large contribution to better community relations and public peace.

The three Labour members brought a useful new element into parliamentary politics. The Labour movement in Ulster had indeed been paralysed by the political and religious divisions of workers and by lack of a local nucleating centre. Of 71 trade unions functioning in Northern Ireland in 1927, when a Trades Disputes Act was passed, 53 were based in Britain. In many respects the Labour movement in the province had been made up of disparate and overlapping bodies or extensions from somewhere else.

The final settlement of the boundary question and a friendly agreement with the government of the Free State greatly relaxed the atmosphere at the close of 1925. Indeed the Dublin government had come to be much more sympathetically viewed by northerners, for it too had had a long fight with I.R.A. extremists.

Some political issues of the period now seem unreal. Protestant puritanism caused some of the churches to put heavy pressure on the government for severely restrictive legislation against the trade in alcoholic drinks and for 'local option' against public houses. The government stonewalled this movement, and it faded out of active politics with the heavy defeat of three 'local option' candidates in the general election of 1929.

In a province where religion has played a major part, it was significant that the extreme fundamentalist wing of the Presbyterians suffered a big setback in 1927 when heresy charges brought against a professor at the Presbyterian Assembly's College, who was held to be a 'modernist', were dismissed by overwhelming majorities at the General Assembly. The event showed that Protestant Christianity in Ulster had moved far in a liberal direction. In the eighteenth and nineteenth centuries there had been liberal or 'non-subscribing' secessions from the main Presbyterian body; but the several small secessions which took place in the twentieth century were of fundamentalist groups which found the Presbyterian Church too liberal or too innovatingly 'modernist' for their taste.

In 1929 proportional representation was abolished and Northern Ireland elections were placed on a basis of single-member constituencies. This had little effect on the larger parties. Full parliamentary franchise had been extended to all women of twenty-one years and upwards in 1928. The foundation of the new parliament buildings at Stormont was laid in 1928 and the building was opened by the Prince of Wales in 1932.

By 1930, ten years from the Act of 1920, much of the subsequent shape of things in Northern Ireland seemed hopefully established. But the province was not prospering materially. There was an average of 59,305 unemployed that year against a total of 267,700 insured persons. One of the two Belfast shipbuilding firms, Workman Clarke, had succumbed; but the other, Harland and Wolff, had in that year the biggest output of any shipbuilding firm in the world.

9. Jurisdiction—Eire Claim Repudiated

'His Majesty's Government in the United Kingdom cannot recognise that the adoption of the name Eire or Ireland involves any right to territory or jurisdiction over territory forming part of the United Kingdom of Great Britain and Northern Ireland, or affects in any way the position of Northern Ireland as an integral part of the United Kingdom'.

The 1930's saw a changed mood in Northern Ireland. Though the difficulties and dangers had not all been dissipated, there was now a well established confidence. In a number of subtle ways the city of Belfast was acquiring some of the qualities of a capital city. Some of its institutional deficiencies were being made good. An art gallery and museum had been opened at Stranmillis in 1929. The parliament buildings at Stormont were opened in 1932. Through the city the once refuse-littered mud banks of the River Lagan were tidied up, a lock and weir were built to keep the water level constant, and broad boulevards laid out along the riverside. The new teachers' training college, the large new public elementary schools through the city, improvements to roads, the removal of the shells of houses wrecked in 'the Troubles', the renewal of many business premises, all helped to induce a new feeling of getting more abreast with the contemporary world.

Belfast began to experiment more with small theatres, with art exhibitions of new kinds. It even began to know itself as a city about which people sometimes wrote novels or essays. The novels of Forrest Reid, the essays of Robert Lynd, the plays of St. John Ervine, the thrillers of F. L. Green or the paintings of William Conor, all stimulated a young generation to think that they also could write and otherwise express themselves originally about the place they grew up in and the people they knew. Since 1924, a local broadcasting station had increasingly made use of local talent and, at first very cautiously, pursued local themes.

In the later 1920's Sir Richard Livingstone, the classical scholar and enthusiastic proponent of adult education, was vice-chancellor of Queen's University, Belfast; and he made quite a habit on public occasions of likening Belfast and Northern Ireland to one of the Greek city states, a community formed by a city with its hinterland. Northern Ireland was small enough to enable anybody of talent to emerge and be taken notice of. People of even quite modest attainments could have the encouragement sometimes of seeing their names in print in Belfast's four daily newspapers. In Northern Ireland, it was possible, as they said, to be a big fish in a small pool. But the province was also large enough and populous enough to confront any aspirant with stimulating competition.

In this cultural expansion of student debates, little magazines, discussion groups, drama groups, art clubs and individual self-expression, there was not much place for the older divisions of creed or politics. Through these interests and pursuits there was release from the inward-turned neurotic self-absorption which the province's troubles and pressures had undoubtedly induced. And these were not for the most part movements of escape. In the first solemn institutional efforts in the 1920's to bring cultural 'sweetness and light' to Ulster there had been a tendency to treat 'culture' as necessarily a wholly different world from what happened in the streets. The activities of the I.R.A. or the huge parades of Orangemen on each Twelfth of July had for years been virtually ignored by local radio, even in news bulletins. In the 1930's these came to be recognised as part of the real human scene, to be talked about with candour and curiosity.

On the political side, however, there were ominous developments. The successful conclusion of the 1925 treaty had given several years of stability and reduced tension; but no effort had been made either by Dublin or Belfast to activate the provisions which that treaty contained for consultation between governments. To say that such discussions would have produced many useful effects is not just to be wise after the event. Even at the time, failure to use the 1925 agreement positively was an obvious failure of statesmanship.

The Dublin government was itself under pressure. It had had the hard and unromantic task of reimposing normality upon a country which had been in a state of anarchy and had been torn by civil war. To the Irish public, with their new sense of independent nationhood, there was something rather boring about the new Free State government's unspectacular but undoubted success. At first there had been little parliamentary opposition in Dail Eireann; but once Eamonn De Valera, the leader of the anti-Treaty side in the civil war, had decided to accept the constitutional situation as he found it and had abandoned the anxious scruples which had caused him to refrain from attending the Dail to which he had been elected, then there existed the nucleus of a possible alternative government party. With a more nationalistic mood developing in the country, the government of the Free State would have found it increasingly difficult to open negotiations with the Northern Ireland government once the first few years had passed after 1925. Opinion in Northern Ireland was very sensitive to what happened in the Free State, and events there were often quickly counterproductive in Northern Ireland. Thus in 1931, when the I.R.A. set about suppressing a meeting of Orangemen in Co Cavan in the Free State, there was an angry reaction in the north, with rioting in Armagh, Lisburn and Portglenone as well as in Belfast. Between 60 and 70 people were injured.

In March, 1932, De Valera and his Fianna Fail party won a general election and took office as the government of the Free State. The new government at once proceeded to default on payments to be made under several financial agreements which their predecessors had made with the United Kingdom. Legislation to abolish the oath of allegiance was introduced and the office of governor general of the Free State, which in a fairly remote way represented the King in the country's constitution, was subjected to a series of calculated slights. What gave point to the symbolic significance of these acts was the fact that they came after and not before the passing of the Statute of Westminster which had released the dominion members of the Commonwealth from control by United Kingdom legislation. The policy of De Valera and his government was to emphasise the purely external nature of the relationship with the United Kingdom and they did not want to seem to be using any enabling power conferred on them by a British statute. On the contrary they sought to assert what they held to be a right existing for all time.

In the atmosphere of controversy arising from the advent of De Valera to power in Dublin, tempers became edgy in Northern Ireland. When the Roman Catholic church held a Eucharistic congress in Dublin in 1932, Protestant hooligans, apparently imagining this event to be a sort of pontificial endorsement of De Valera's policy, attacked excursionists going to the congress as they passed through Ballymena, Portadown and Larne Harbour. In October there were riots in Belfast in which two persons were killed and many injured.

Politicians were also edgy and nervous and inclined to talk wildly. To this period belong several exceptional and adversely quotable remarks made by a few prominent people in Northern Ireland. Among them was a particularly well-known one from Sir James Craig, the Prime Minister, about 'a Protestant parliament for a Protestant people'. This and several others like it from other people at that time have often been quoted as if they were the embodiment of a philosophy; but they belong to the nervous and vituperative atmosphere of the early 1930's, and one does not find comparable sayings from people of comparable importance in earlier or later times.

In the spring of 1933 the Dublin government made it possible for the I.R.A. to resume many of its public activities. Meetings held by De Valera's opponents were broken up with violence. In alarm his opponents sought the aid of another organisation, the Army Comrades Associations, which was later renamed the National Guard and popularly known from its uniform as the Blue Shirts. It was led by General Eoin O'Duffy, who later led a force of Irish Volunteers to support General Franco in the Spanish civil war.

As tempers frayed in the Free State, republican activities increased greatly in Northern Ireland. There were attacks on individuals and on buildings, secret or even fairly open military drilling, incitements to outrage and the distribution of seditious literature. Some republicans were interned and others expelled across the frontier.

It was in 1935, however, that the most serious riots for many years occurred in Belfast. In May there were disorderly scenes in Belfast, with hand grenades thrown and a man shot. A police sergeant was wounded in June. Early in July three persons received bullet wounds. Later in July there were serious riots in which nine persons died. A curfew was imposed for a short period and the army called in to assist in keeping order. The old pattern reasserted itself. The majority of those shot were Protestants but those who were the victims of burning, looting and window smashing were mainly Roman Catholics.

Events quite remote from the British Isles also caused divisions of feeling from 1936. The Spanish civil war evoked in Ulster cordial Protestant sympathy for the constitutional government of Spain, while Roman Catholics generally tended to sympathise with the insurgents under General Franco and with his fascist allies. Through 1936 the police were kept busy by underground republican activities in Belfast and elsewhere. The I.R.A. had many friends in America, and in that year 400 Thomson machine guns were imported by republicans from the United States.

These and other arms, ammunition and explosives began to enter Northern Ireland in large quantities.

The police made some use of special powers to institute searches and question individuals. In 1936 the National Council for Civil Liberties published a report of a commission of enquiry into the working of special powers in Northern Ireland. It drew attention particularly to those aspects of special powers legislation which could result in arrest and imprisonment without trial, a matter which must be of grave concern to anybody who has a care for safe and civilised living. But the report adduced very meagre evidence to demonstrate any abuse of special powers. By this time the Dublin government had found the I.R.A. getting so much out of hand that strong measures were taken to restrain it. These measures included the adoption of special powers similar to those available to government in Northern Ireland.

The political trends of those years in the Free State found their culmination in the adoption by plebiscite in 1937 of a constitution of largely republican form. The old name of the Free State was abandoned and the title of Eire was now adopted for general use. For Northern Ireland the important aspect of this constitution was that it claimed to be for the whole of Ireland. According to it, Northern Ireland as a political entity was non-existent. The treaty of 1925 was completely ignored and with it was thrown away any notion or prospect of generous and friendly negotiation and co-operation between north and south.

The events of the internal politics of Eire during the 1930's, the episode of the Blue Shirts and other developments, had, moreover, destroyed any element on the opposition benches of the Dail which might have carried on the tradition, established between W. T. Cosgrave and Sir James Craig, of friendly discussion between the governments in Belfast and Dublin. Ireland had also become more deeply divided in another way. Until De Valera and his party came into power, the frontier between north and south, or the sea frontier between the Free State and Britain, was only administrative. Only to a small degree was it an economic frontier. Now, through a policy of protective tariffs adopted as part of an 'economic war' against Britain, the frontier had become a formidable economic barrier of a kind that would have been particularly disastrous to Northern Ireland if that province had been placed inside it instead of remaining fortunately outside it. The position of Northern Ireland thus became that of a small country against which a larger neighbour was making a total and unqualified irredentist claim. This is always a dangerous and demoralising situation. Historical parallels are nearly always misleading. One that was evidently in the mind of the Ulster Prime Minister was the case of Czechoslovakia, under irredentist pressure from Germany and at last ruined and cut up under the Munich agreement. In a speech of that period, Lord Craigavon said, 'Ulster is nobody's Czechoslovakia'.

Like Czechoslovakia, Northern Ireland had a minority, and from now on a steady effort was made to use this minority in a subversive sense. As in Czechoslovakia, too, the minority in Northern Ireland had been particularly affected by unemployment and it had many real grievances. These had also been intensified by the fact that the persistent claim from across the frontier had been strongly counterproductive and caused the minority in Northern Ireland to feel from time to time the effects of a reactive Protestant backlash.

Up to the time of writing, that irredentist claim has remained embodied in the constitution of the Irish Republic and, though it has been pursued with less energy or confidence in later years, it has created a considerable feeling of unease in Northern Ireland which has risen from time to time into a more or less serious crisis.

The United Kingdom government repudiated the claim embodied in the new constitution of Eire and issued a statement containing the following words:

'His Majesty's government in the United Kingdom take note of Articles 2, 3 and 4 of the new constitution. They cannot recognise that the adoption of the name 'Eire' or 'Ireland' or any other provision of those articles, involves any right to territory or jurisdiction over territory forming part of the United Kingdom of Great Britain and Northern Ireland, or affects in any way the position of Northern Ireland as an integral part of the United Kingdom of Great Britain and Northern Ireland. They therefore regard the use of the name 'Eire' or 'Ireland' in this connection as relating only to that area which has hitherto been known as the Irish Free State.'

10. War and Peace

'But for the loyalty of Northern Ireland and its devotion to what has now become the cause of thirty governments or nations, we should have been confronted with slavery and death, and the light which now shines so strongly throughout the world would have been quenched.' Winston Churchill.

The late 1930s were restless years in Northern Ireland. Industry was depressed and unemployment extremely heavy. In 1938 the province's total visible exports were estimated at a mere £51,061,000. In that year there were 347,850 insured persons, and there was an average unemployment rate for the year of 90,675. To be unemployed at that time was depressing and demoralising but not as grim as in the 1920s. A series of agreements about finance had kept Northern Ireland's standards of social services and benefit payments level with those in Britain. An Unemployment Act on the same lines as similar legislation in Britain had been adopted in 1934 and it had been agreed that unemployment benefit should be the same as in Britain.

In 1937 it had been agreed that if a deficit occurred in the Northern Ireland budget which was not due to higher standards of social expenditure than in Britain, this could be made good in some way with the help of the United Kingdom government. In the same year it was agreed that agricultural subsidies were to be extended to Northern Ireland in the same way as in Britain. The doctrine was thus being fully established that Northern Ireland must be given as high a standard of aid and welfare as any other part of the United Kingdom and that the Northern Ireland government might initiate any developments in these fields up to the level of similar developments in Britain.

The prosperity of the province was necessarily bound up with that of the whole United Kingdom, and its overseas trade was the concern of the United Kingdom government. But, justly or unjustly, much dissatisfaction in the province tended to be directed at the government of Northern Ireland in the first instance. Apart from the economic stagnation, there were other causes for a growing impatience with the government of the province. Over the years that government had increasingly tried to encourage the quality and productivity of both industry and agriculture. The initial Marketing of Eggs Act of 1924 had been followed by a series of rather similar acts which pushed up the quality and marketing standards of a wide range of agricultural produce. In 1932 also came the first of a long series of acts designed to induce by means of easy loans and other advantages the establishment of new industries in the province. In 1935 the Northern Ireland government tried to deal with another economic problem by a virtual nationalisation of a great part of the province's road transport system.

All these efforts produced their results, but not rapid or spectacular results; and the public remained impatient and inclined in some quarters to be derisive. Nevertheless an examination of particular issues shows that again and again the cabinet and front bench were rather to the 'left' or on the progressive side of their own back benches. In 1938 one of the Ulster Unionist members at Westminster, W. J. Stewart, a building contractor, member for South Belfast, founded a Progressive Unionist Party. With a piecemeal policy, partly progressive, partly reactionary, and attacking the government's extensive school-building policy, the new party expressed a mood of frustration that was widespread in the province. In a general election in 1938 the Progressive Unionists won many votes but no seats and soon faded from the political scene. But they were a significant symptom of the mood of the province at the time.

In 1939 came the Second World War. Northern Ireland entered the war as part of the United Kingdom. Eire remained at peace and so was neutral. The wartime neutrality of Eire was to have much influence upon Northern Ireland. Under the Articles of Agreement of 1921 certain ports and bases in Eire were reserved for British use for defence purposes; but in an agreement of 1938 the British government had renounced control and use of these ports and bases. In the First World War, Irish ports had been of great importance for the protection of Atlantic shipping. Now in the Second World War the whole protective role of Irish bases had to be concentrated in Northern Ireland under conditions which were to make the fulfilment of this role far more desperately crucial than before.

The outbreak of war drew the whole community together in Northern Ireland. The wartime legislation and special administrative arrangements which applied to Britain applied equally to Northern Ireland. In some cases departments of the Northern Ireland government acted as agents in the province for the corresponding departments of various United Kingdom ministries in carrying out the various special tasks which wartime conditions required. A major exception to this legislative and administrative uniformity with Britain was, however, the fact that conscription of manpower was not imposed on the province. The conscription question was raised on several occasions, particularly in May 1941, but the United Kingdom government turned the project down, apparently for two main reasons. First they wished to avoid offending the minority in the province who might be thought to share the neutral sentiments of Eire. Secondly, conscription would have disturbed the labour situation in a province which had been highly organised as a productive asset and was producing a very high output of food from small family farms. Winston Churchill summed the matter up in the House of Commons by saying that it would be 'more trouble than it is worth to enforce such a policy' in Northern Ireland.

It is not possible to separate the figures for voluntary recruitment for the services in Northern Ireland from those in the rest of the United Kingdom. There were, of course, many Ulstermen already in the armed services; and a very large number joined territorial units in the months just before war broke out, particularly in artillery. Actual wartime recruitment was thus diminished by the extent of heavy anticipatory recruitment immediately before the war. It has been suggested that recruitment during the war itself was about 38,000.

While Ulster people took part individually in nearly every battle and campaign of the war, by land, sea and air, there were certain land campaigns in which actual Ulster units took part. The opening phase of the war in France, ending in the Dunkirk evacuation, the brief landing in Norway in 1940, the campaigns in North Africa, Burma, Sicily and Italy, the Normandy landings, the Allied advance to the Rhine and into Germany, all saw Ulstermen serving together either as members of battalions of the several old Ulster regiments or in other units. A high proportion were in artillery or with mobile armoured units. Individuals from Ulster also served in all the British forces and some also in Commonwealth forces or in the United States services.

A very high proportion of British commanders were men of Ulster birth or came from Ulster families—men such as Field Marshals Dill, Auchinleck, Alanbrooke, Alexander and Montgomery, and General Templar who later became a Field Marshal. Indeed field marshals and successive chiefs of the Imperial General Staff were for a while a major Ulster 'export'.

During this period there was some natural anxiety about the safety of Northern Ireland itself. The endemic trouble with the I.R.A. became increasingly formidable as the war proceeded. Plans were laid by members of the I.R.A. to sabotage the civil defence system and the fire service, shoot the police and aid the Germans in the event of their invading the island. During the war eighty-two illicit dumps of arms were discovered in Northern Ireland and special powers were used to detain and intern suspects, nearly all of whom freely admitted to being members of the I.R.A. About a hundred were prosecuted and tried in the ordinary courts and nearly all stated that they were members of the I.R.A. and refused to recognise the authority of the court.

This groping underground warfare with the I.R.A. required much vigilance and involved many people throughout the war. The Ulster Special Constabulary, which had consisted of 13,000 men at the outbreak of war, was expanded for Home Guard duties to a force exceeding 40,000 but was reduced to 10,000 when the war ended.

Another cause of anxiety in Ulster was the possibility of proposals of a character very unpalatable to the people of Northern Ireland being made by the British government to persuade the government of Eire to enter the war. It is now known that, under the extreme pressure of wartime peril, the British government did actually make unsuccessful approaches to the Dublin government.

When the crisis came in 1940 and Britain was isolated against the resources of a great part of western Europe, Lord Craigavon himself declared the readiness of his government to co-operate fully with Eire, provided Eire came into the war as Britain's ally and raised no constitutional issues.

However, De Valera predictably refused to let his country be drawn into the war. It has sometimes since been stated that the wartime neutrality of Eire was the result of the partition of Ireland and the establishment of a separate government of Northern Ireland; but this was not the view expressed at the time by De Valera as head of the government of Eire. In an interview in November 1940, he said, 'We are entitled to freedom as well as unity—and there is no more important matter in which that freedom can be exercised than in the choice of peace or war. To suggest that the undoing of partition might be made dependent on our going into this war is to fail to understand our whole position.'

The collapse of France, Belgium and the Netherlands and the great crisis of 1940 gave Northern Ireland a crucial strategic role as the base protecting Britain's Atlantic approaches. Many new airfields were quickly made, to facilitate the air cover to be given out at sea, and Belfast Lough was much used for marshalling convoys of shipping. The relative remoteness of the province from air striking range of the continent caused it to be used also for training, storage and many other strategic purposes. The chamber which houses the senate at the Parliament House at Stormont became an R.A.F. operations room. And always in the background the Royal Ulster Constabulary, the Ulster Special Constabulary and other local defence and security bodies tried to forestall and prevent the efforts of the I.R.A. to disrupt the strategic activities which went on in the province.

By many it was rather assumed that Belfast would escape the attentions of the Luftwaffe; but on the night of 15–16 April 1941, after a brief probing raid a few days before, there came the first long night of bombing. Defences were very limited. There were in Northern Ireland only 24 heavy and 14 light anti-aircraft guns, a squadron of Hurricane fighters, one bomb disposal unit and two small balloon barrage units. The attackers had things largely their own way. An early chance hit wrecked the telephone communication system on which the guns depended, and after that the bombs continued but the guns almost ceased. According to the German official report, 180 planes participated. A large proportion of the bombs and parachute mines fell on residential areas and many buildings were set on fire. As the situation got quite beyond the capacity of the province's fire services, thirteen fire engines drove through the night across the frontier from Dublin, Drogheda, Dundalk and Dun Laoghaire to help. The next day fire pumps were brought by sea, 10 from Liverpool and 32 from Glasgow. There were over 700 dead and over 400 serious casualties.

The police and the civil defence personnel remained wonderfully steady through these experiences, for which they were very unprepared both materially and psychologically, and they did what had to be done. There had been very little evacuation of school children before the raids; but it was always easy to go out of the city into the adjacent country, and many people now did so. There was a strange chaotic intermingling of townspeople among country people, the social effects of which linger to this day.

A further prolonged and destructive night of bombing came to Belfast on 4–5 May. It produced fewer deaths, only around 150, but did grave damage to shipyards and aircraft factory and other industrial establishments and started many destructive fires. After that there were no more air raids. It was estimated that 53,000 houses had been damaged, 4,000 of them very badly, and 3,200 totally destroyed.

Early in 1942 the first United States forces in the European theatre began to arrive in Northern Ireland which became a bridgehead for the deployment of American forces. Originally it had been optimistically hoped that the Americans would be allowed to land in Eire, but Eire remained resolutely neutral. The coming of great numbers of Americans, with vast quantities of armoured vehicles and equipment, was very spectacular and for a while they seemed to be ubiquitous in Northern Ireland and produced a marked social impact wherever they went. Then they moved on, some to take part in the North African landings and some to land in Normandy; but substantial American forces were using Northern Ireland as a transit base during the remainder of the war.

Under the surface of these events the life of Northern Ireland went on rather much as in peacetime but at a pace and pressure set by the needs of production. The province turned out 140 warships, a tenth of all the merchant shipping of the United Kingdom, guns, tanks, ammunition, aircraft, including 1,500 heavy bombers, much miscellaneous machinery, two million parachutes, 90 per cent of the service shirts required for the British forces, one-third of the ropes required for War Office purposes and many other strategic products. In addition much production of a peacetime character went on for export to gain credit abroad. In particular, linen and whiskey were important means of earning dollars, Ulster linen being the United Kingdom's second biggest overseas trading asset. And the farmers of Northern Ireland made a larger proportionate contribution to the home-produced food supply than those of any other area of the British Isles. The war changed Northern Ireland in many ways. It gave many younger people experience abroad in the services. It gave rise to many marriages with people from other countries, including many Americans. It led to a large re-equipment of several important sectors of the province's industry. It changed farming. The end of the war, for example, saw ten times as many tractors in use in the fields of Northern Ireland as there had been at its beginning.

Politically the war emphasised the contrasting and diverging destinies that had been chosen by the northern and southern communities in Ireland. On the other hand it created many opportunities for contacts and exchanges at a purely personal level. Many Ulster people took to spending occasional holidays in Dublin, to gaze at the peacetime scene there and buy goods rationed or unobtainable at home. And many southerners emigrated from their own country to take up civilian work in Britain or in Northern Ireland or to join the British services in which some of them served with great distinction.

The war also created the opportunity at last for a new generation to take over the government of Northern Ireland. Lord Craigavon died in the early winter of 1940 and was succeeded as Prime Minister by Mr. J. M. Andrews, formerly his Minister of Finance. Lord Craigavon had been very much the grand old man of Ulster politics, respected with good reason by all, including his most active opponents. His passing was the signal for a big change in the political scene, Andrews gave way in 1943 to Sir Basil Brooke, who formed a new and much younger cabinet. Among the members of it he included Mr. H. C. Midgley. Midgley had long been chairman of the Northern Ireland Labour Party but, in reaction against the republican sympathies of some of his colleagues in that party, had broken away from it to form the Commonwealth Labour Party. He now joined the government as Minister of Public Security.

On his retirement from the office of Prime Minister, Andrews received a letter from Winston Churchill in which the latter referred to the vital strategic role which Northern Ireland had fulfilled in the crisis of the war and said, 'But for the loyalty of Northern Ireland and its devotion to what has now become the cause of thirty governments or nations, we should have been confronted with slavery and death, and the light which now shines so strongly throughout the world would have been quenched.'

11. Welfare State: Industrial Development

'Time has shown that the efforts of the Northern Ireland Government have been very successful in attracting new industries of a substantial and well established character. Many British and American and several German and other continental firms have invested in a wide variety of enterprises in Northern Ireland.'

Two major themes dominated the social and economic history of Northern Ireland during the years which followed the close of the second World War. One was the establishment in the province of the full machinery of the 'welfare state'. The other was the unfoldment of a remarkably successful policy of state-aided industrial renewal and development.

The Westminster general election of 1945 brought into office the Labour government of Mr. Attlee, which was firmly resolved to give effective implementation to the project of a comprehensive national health and social security scheme such as had been laid before the preceding government in the Beveridge report.

The advent of a strong Labour government in Britain brought to the testing certain unwritten elements in the constitution of Northern Ireland; for the historical circumstances of the province had always kept in office at Stormont a Unionist government, and the Ulster Unionist party was affiliated to the Conservative party in Britain. The small Ulster parliamentary representation at Westminster was also very largely and sometimes exclusively Unionist and normally sat and voted with the Conservatives.

The Northern Ireland government was bound to cooperate very substantially in some of the policies of any government in power at Westminster when those policies concerned the United Kingdom as a whole and involved Northern Ireland. Even in matters which might seem wholly internal to Northern Ireland, the province could not afford to be seriously out of step with what was being done throughout the rest of the United Kingdom. Northern Ireland could move out of strict conformity but not into actual disharmony with what was being done in Britain.

In the event, the Northern Ireland government of Sir Basil Brooke—later Lord Brookeborough—established a very friendly and co-operative relationship with the Attlee government at Westminster. Yet many saw it as a paradox that the Unionist government in Northern Ireland in due course introduced legislation applying to Northern Ireland the same social policies which the Unionist members at Westminster had joined with their Conservative colleagues in voting against. The paradox was certainly much less emphatic than it seemed, for neither major political party in Britain rejected the general principle of a welfare state, and the Beveridge report had been accepted by the predominantly Conservative government of Mr. Churchill. What was voted on at Westminster was more the question of what sort of government one wanted to see applying the policy, and with what shades of emphasis. Experience had shown that when a group of a dozen or fewer Ulster Unionist members had gone to Westminster to represent the interests of Northern Ireland, there was really no other course open to them as a group than to affiliate with one of the major political parties. And, though the Labour party has been very sympathetic towards the special needs of Northern Ireland and, when in office, has been financially generous to the province, the Unionists always felt that there was a more uniformly diffused understanding of their needs in the Conservative party with which they had been historically associated for several generations.

The historical roots of an element of some antipathy towards Ulster Unionism are easy to find in the Labour movement. Unionism in one of its aspects, particularly in the nineteenth century, had been a movement favoured by the landlord class in Ireland, and this was bound to alienate many Labour sympathisers. Then, in many respects, Labour in Britain had inherited some of the role and tradition of the old Liberal party which came to disaster through its handling of Irish problems and had found Ulster a particularly indigestible element among those problems.

But one of the most powerful factors in deterring the Labour party in Britain from a wholeheartedly cordial relationship with Ulster Unionists was the presence in many British constituencies of a large southern Irish immigrant vote.

During half a century nearly a million people emigrated from the south of Ireland and a large proportion of these carried with them the traditional nationalist sentiments of the Republic and constituted a powerful pressure group.

At the same time the political atmosphere of Northern Ireland had long been very radical. Before the future of the Union was put in question by Gladstone, Ulster was represented at Westminster by a strong group of Liberal members. Three-quarters of a century of separation from the radical wing of British politics did not destroy the instinctive radicalism of many Ulster people.

This confused pattern of political cross currents formed the background to the cordial co-operation which developed between the Attlee government at Westminster and the Brooke government at Stormont. With some very minor adjustments to suit local conditions, the full range of welfare, health and national insurance schemes introduced in Britain was reproduced in Northern Ireland and was in operation from 1948.

A fear closely connected with the establishment of the improved welfare standards and services in Northern Ireland was that they would cause a great influx of immigrants from across the frontier, desiring to seek employment under the better conditions of Northern Ireland. In 1947 a Safeguarding of Employment Act introduced a permit system covering immigrant labour in certain types of employment, chiefly those in which there was already unemployment in the province. No permits were required for self-employed persons, teachers of any kind, long residents, natives or their spouses.

Northern Ireland had kept in step with British social legislation in another respect by introducing in 1947 an education act which was the equivalent of the British wartime 'Butler Act' and provided state financed education for all, according to their needs, in primary, secondary modern and grammar schools, and provided also for university and other higher education for those who could benefit by it. The same advantages were provided for those pursuing their education in the Roman Catholic school system which ran parallel to but completely separate from the ordinary public education system.

Other efforts to deal with the social side of government responsibility in Northern Ireland included the establishment of a Northern Ireland Housing Trust, financed by the government, to build houses either directly or as agent for local authorities. This imaginative experiment in nationalised home building was very successful and did much to put Northern Ireland slightly ahead of Britain in the proportion of its families to be found in post-war homes twenty years later.

The Conservatism of Ulster Unionists did not specially favour nationalisation schemes but equally had no doctrinaire inhibitions against them when applied usefully to public utility services such as electricity. A variety of experiments in nationalised transport under the administrations of Lord Craigavon and Lord Brookeborough ended under the subsequent O'Neill administration with transport being administered by private operators under licence, a restoration of private enterprise but not an uncontrolled 'free for all'.

The financing of the greatly expanded range of government responsibilities in Northern Ireland proceeded on the principles which had already been in operation before the war. The principle that Northern Ireland should have parity with the rest of the United Kingdom in social services was extended to all the new services carried on under the welfare state. Most of the cost of such services was, of course, met out of the proceeds of taxation in Northern Ireland or out of the contributions of insured persons, but the post-war world was in many respects a world of bigger budgets, and the financial nexus between Northern Ireland and Britain became much larger and more significant.

This brought more into prominence during the following years, and sometimes into controversy, the question of how far Britain was subsidising Northern Ireland. Of course the individual in Northern Ireland was paying just as much in taxation as his fellow citizens in Britain and was receiving the same benefit payments as his neighbour in Great Britain and an equitable share of other exchequer expenditure. Many areas in the United Kingdom undoubtedly receive rather more in terms of exchequer expenditure than they can contribute by way of taxation, only the more prosperous areas such as the Midlands and South East of England contributing substantially more in taxation than they receive in government expenditure. But Northern Ireland has always been placed in the unique position of having this fact demonstrated visibly and in detail in public accounts, whereas in other places it is very hard or impossible to say exactly how the balance of receipt and contribution is working.

Figures ranging from £65 million to £100 million have been commonly used in recent years to indicate the extent of the financial support, direct and indirect, which the Northern Ireland Exchequer derives from the United Kingdom Exchequer. The precise amount of this 'subsidy' depends on how subsidy is defined. In October 1969 the Treasury published estimates which implied that in 1967–68 Scotland was 'subsidised' to the extent of £341 million, which is equivalent to about £68 per head of population. These figures (themselves the subject of some controversy) cannot be compared directly with those just quoted for Northern Ireland because they were compiled on a different basis. Their relevance is that they illustrate the general point that Northern Ireland is not the only region of the United Kingdom which derives a net benefit from the United Kingdom Exchequer.

But this is not the whole picture. Government finance is only one, and not the largest, of three kinds of financial flow taking place between Britain and Northern Ireland. The other two are, first, investment and the profits from investment, and, secondly, trade. Much industry and property in Northern Ireland pays profits to owners and shareholders in Britain, and Northern Ireland production and trade have long been a British asset in world trade and a support to Britain's international balance of payments position. A high proportion of the goods exported from Northern Ireland to Britain are and have always been goods in transit, destined to form part of Britain's export trade.

The notion undoubtedly arose in the post-war years that, because people in Northern Ireland, who paid the same taxes as people in Britain, were given social services as good as those in Britain, Northern Ireland was necessarily a financial drag on Britain. But at government level the fallacious nature of much that was put forward on these lines was well understood, and the financial relations between the central government and the provincial government continued smoothly on the lines which had been largely established in the 1920s by the Colwyn Committee.

Alongside the establishment of the welfare state in Northern Ireland went an increasingly adventurous policy of state-aided industrial renewal. The first efforts to encourage re-equipment and diversification of industry had been made before the war. Acts of 1932 and 1937 made grants and loans available to meet the cost of acquiring sites and erecting, purchasing, renovating or adapting premises for industrial use. Local authorities were empowered to exempt new industries from local government taxation for a limited period. The most important new undertakings established under these earlier acts were concerned with aircraft manufacture.

After the war came a series of new acts to extend this policy. The government was empowered to provide financial assistance, not only to industry but to local authorities and public utility bodies where these could assist industrial development by improvement of roads, water, sewerage and power services. Grants and loans were made for expenditure on buildings and plant and the cost of moving and installing machinery. The policy of giving grants was preferred to that of advancing loans.

To speed up the establishment of new industries, a further scheme was adopted of building and leasing or selling new factories to new enterprises. These state-built 'off-the-peg' factories were such a novel and boldly pushful idea that they attracted widespread interest. Up to the time of writing, almost fourteen million square feet of government-built factory space have been provided and put into use in the province. These plans to extend and diversify the province's manufacturing industries necessarily depended for much of their success on the foresight, energy and adroitness of the staff of the Ministry of Commerce and of successive ministers in seeking out and negotiating with industrial concerns able and likely to establish undertakings in the province. In this they were much aided by the compactness and mobility of the whole administration of Northern Ireland; for other departments of government were able when necessary to facilitate new enterprises in a way that could not have been possible in a larger or more remotely controlled administration. It was always possible for the interested industrialist to see the man at the top and obtain prompt decisions and have special adjustments made to suit his needs. Administrations in other countries which have paid Northern Ireland the compliment of imitation have not been able to equal the Ulster government in these respects.

There were, of course, disappointments in the form of firms coming to the province only for a short period and then leaving. But time has shown that the efforts of the Northern Ireland government have been very successful in attracting new industries of a substantial and well established character. Many British and American and several German and other continental firms have invested in a wide variety of enterprises in Northern Ireland, establishing branches of existing undertakings or completely new and independent industries; and most of them have had good reason for satisfaction with their ventures in the province, where there is a good labour force and excellent facilities of many kinds. In particular the province has been given the biggest complex of synthetic fibre and textile industries in Europe.

In the twenty years prior to the time of writing, the government has in these ways succeeded in creating 77,000 new jobs in Northern Ireland in manufacturing industry. These jobs employ nearly two-fifths of the province's entire manufacturing labour force of over 186,000.

Emphasis on the government's work in industrial renewal must not be taken as implying any lack of enterprise on the part of firms and individuals in the province, where a very high level of inventiveness and adaptability was shown in both new and long established industries. It is not possible here to refer to particular examples; but, at the time, an example of ingenious Ulster canniness which caught and amused the interest of the press and public was a very small engineering firm in Northern Ireland which took to manufacturing boomerangs and exporting them successfully to Australia.

The unemployment problem of Northern Ireland was much mitigated but not solved by the government's policies; for much of the new industry was highly automated, giving fewer jobs in relation to productivity than in the past. Education and training schemes and efforts to up-grade labour into more skilled categories have therefore been another important aspect of the province's economic strategy.

Northern Ireland has seemed to be burdened with certain almost irreducible types of unemployment in the form of casual unskilled labourers in rural areas and small towns, unwilling to move in pursuit of work. Employment in agriculture has steadily fallen as farms have become larger and fewer and have been more rationalised and mechanised in their administration and cultivation. In the quarter of a century following the close of the Second World War, the number of farms in Northern Ireland has been halved. At the time of writing they produce seven per cent of the value of the United Kingdom's total agricultural gross output, including 30 per cent of the United Kingdom's production of bacon, 14 per cent of fat cattle and 12 per cent of eggs.

Another industry which extended considerably in the post-war period was tourism, and in expanding it introduced new social influences from outside. The province's rich scenic, coastal and recreational attractions came to be much more widely known, and a government tourist board endeavoured to bring about improved amenities.

On the political side Northern Ireland seemed to run fairly smoothly in the years of Lord Brookeborough's government. At general elections his Unionist party held between 33 and 38 of the 52 seats in the Northern Ireland House of Commons. The voting situation in the province, however, was sometimes most clearly shown in the elections for the twelve Westminster seats, for in the Stormont elections there was normally quite a high proportion of uncontested seats. Thus in 1955, ten years after the end of the war, all twelve Ulster Westminster seats were contested both by Unionists and by Sinn Fein candidates. The Unionists obtained 68.5 per cent of the total vote, winning ten seats, and Sinn Fein obtained 23.5 per cent, winning two seats, the remaining percentage of votes going to Labour and one other candidate. When a similar contest took place in 1959, with Unionists and Sinn Fein again contesting all seats, the Unionists got 77.2 per cent of the votes and Sinn Fein only 11 per cent, while the Unionists won every seat. In 1964, when Unionist and Republican candidates contested every seat and Labour contested ten of the seats, the distribution of votes was 63 per cent to the Unionists, who again won every seat, 16.1 per cent to Labour and 15.9 per cent to the Republicans.

It is clear from these figures that the maintenance of the Union and of the province's constitutional position as part of the United Kingdom was upheld by a very great majority of the people in the province, and on this issue Lord Brookeborough's government had public opinion strongly on its side. On other matters the Unionist party was much less united and under less discipline than parties normally are in Britain; for, with no opposition party capable of forming a viable alternative government, many of the differences which are fought out between parties in Britain had to be fought out between the right and left wings of the Unionist party at Stormont, or between other groupings which formed from time to time, the government holding a position which was central or sometimes a little left of centre.

In spite of the undoubted strong majority support for the province's constitution, the Dublin government continued after the war to treat Northern Ireland as being *de jure* part of Eire, though admitting that *de facto* it was not. In 1946 Mr. De Valera had said that if he had been at the head of a powerful nation he would not have hesitated to use force to bring Ulster under the rule of his government; and in 1948 he toured the English-speaking world to work up feeling, particularly among Irish expatriots, in favour of the incorporation of Northern Ireland in Eire.

The Attlee government however acted scrupulously in the spirit of Northern Ireland's constitution; and, when the Costello government withdrew the Irish Republic from membership of the Commonwealth, the Ireland Act of 1949 which was passed at Westminster to deal with the consequences of this situation contained the words, 'In no event will Northern Ireland or any part thereof cease to be part of His Majesty's dominions and of the United Kingdom without the consent of the Parliament of Northern Ireland.'

These events and the eclipse of the Northern Ireland Labour party at the 1949 Stormont elections brought that party to a crisis, and in that year, 1949, it adopted a definite policy on the constitution of Northern Ireland, on which it had previously been deeply divided. It pledged itself to 'maintain unbroken the connexion between Great Britain and Northern Ireland as a part of the Commonwealth'.

On the basis of this policy commitment and with the changed position of the Irish Republic, the Northern Ireland Labour party began to improve its fortunes, and by 1958 it had four members in the Northern Ireland parliament, a group which came to enjoy much public respect. It was fulfilling the main duties of a parliamentary opposition and exerting a positive influence on government policy. Hopes were expressed that it would develop into a party capable of one day providing an alternative government. But it failed to hold its own in the face of a wave of popularity evoked by the policies followed in the opening years of the government of Captain O'Neill.

12. Years of Achievement

'In fifty years a backward Province has been transformed by the energy and public spirit of its inhabitants.'

The shared experiences of wartime had begun to draw the community together, and a much more relaxed atmosphere prevailed in those regions of social, religious and 'tribal' differences which had always existed. The Roman Catholic part of the community took a long step forward in prosperity and status. As the Commission headed by Lord Cameron, the Scottish High Court judge, reported in 1969, 'A much larger Catholic middle class has emerged.' Larger numbers of Roman Catholics than hitherto entered the civil service or gave good service to the community in other roles or professions in which previously they had been less fully represented. The new welfare state not only drew attention to the obvious advantages of British citizenship but removed many past hardships and social injustices.

In local government, however, a policy of leaving things largely unchanged had now come to invite justly adverse criticism. The local government electoral boundaries in Northern Ireland had been drawn upon a principle laid down in British law at the time of their establishment, that regard should be had to equality of rateable valuation in the various electoral areas. This caused them to accord inequitably in some places with distribution of population. This was outstandingly the case in the borough of Londonderry. In some parts of Northern Ireland, Roman Catholics felt that they had emphatic grievances against certain predominantly Protestant and Unionist councils; and there were Protestants and Unionists who felt that they had grievances against predominantly Roman Catholic councils.

Probably, however, the deepest frustrations which the minority in Northern Ireland suffered were social and psychological. In large areas of social intercourse both sides were confined within 'closed shops'. The Protestant and Unionist closed shop was a more spacious and comfortable one and those inside it were more at ease in it and clearly felt no strong motive for trying to get out of it. But the Roman Catholic closed shop was much more confining and less comfortable, its restrictive nature being reinforced by a separate education system under Church control. In the top levels of education, in the arts and sciences and some of the professions, there was plenty of social intercourse between these groups and often an almost complete and entirely civilised breaking down of self-conscious barriers. But great bodies of people kept on living within the narrow confines of credal groups, with no friend or close acquaintance in any group but their own, choosing of their own accord to live exclusively in separate streets or housing estates.

In 1961, the last occasion when a census of religious professions was taken, Roman Catholics numbered 497,547. This represented an increase of 26,087 over the 1951 figure. The indication that the rate of increase of the Roman Catholics was slightly faster than the Protestant, added an uneasiness to the situation.

Politically the segregation on religious lines manifested itself in the fact that nearly every Unionist member of parliament was also a member of the Orange Order, while supporting the Nationalist party was a body called the Catholic Voters' Registration Committee. This acute identification of religion and politics had increased during the 1920s and 1930s. In earlier days Sir Edward Carson as leader of the Ulster Unionists had not identified himself with the Orange Order and it had been possible for a Roman Catholic to sit as Unionist member of parliament for a Londonderry seat. Equally Protestants had played prominent roles in Nationalist politics. But the terrorism and bitterness of the 1920s had changed all that, and irredentist efforts from across the frontier had spread a social poison.

Certainly there were dissatisfactions and potentially dangerous tensions in Northern Ireland during those post-war years, and it will always be a matter of speculation how far they could have been adjusted, reduced and 'de-fused'. What seems desirable from hindsight is not, however, always politically possible at the time and the external pressures upon Northern Ireland in those years would almost certainly have prevented such an enterprise as a revision of the local government system from becoming practical politics. It would have met with fierce 'grass roots' resistance and hence with indefinite deferment. The problems of Northern Ireland were not simply internal. Since the placing of the Dublin government on a clearly republican basis and the withdrawal of the Irish Republic from the Commonwealth, there had been unremitting pressure upon Northern Ireland from the province's larger neighbour, and there had been many developments within the Republic highly disturbing to the majority in Ulster.

Northern Protestant spectators of the southern scene were repelled by the substantially different social policies pursued in the south, by the lower standards of living there, by the low level of welfare services and benefit payments, by the actual abandonment in 1951 of a mother and child welfare scheme in deference to the Roman Catholic hierarchy, by the state of the law in the south on divorce, contraception, literary censorship and several other matters, by the much less developed educational facilities and the compulsory learning and use of the Gaelic language in many connections. They viewed with real alarm the notion of their possible incorporation in a state whose economic condition was substantially lower than that of Northern Ireland. Indeed all the reasons which had prompted the northeners to take a different course from the rest of Ireland since the 1880s were still felt to be vigorously operative.

But to many northeners, even more persuasive than these factors was the decline of the Protestant minority in the Irish Republic. Between 1946 and 1961, according to Dublin government figures, there was a fall of over 20 per cent in the number of Presbyterians and Methodists in the Republic and of nearly 17 per cent in the number of Anglicans while the general fall in the population was only four and a half per cent. Although the Protestants in Northern Ireland were in a majority they were deeply conscious of the fact that in Ireland as a whole they were a relatively small minority; and the decline in numbers of their co-religionists under the government of the Republic influenced them very deeply.

The Cameron Commission reporting on the disturbances of 1969 in Northern Ireland said that 'the fears and apprehensions felt widely among Unionists have solid and substantial basis both in the past and even in the present'. In a good-humoured and conciliatory comment on this at the time Mr. Edward McAteer, leader of the Nationalist party, conceded the reality of the Protestant fears and said that they were an aspect of the situation which had not got sufficient attention.

Attitudes in Northern Ireland were even more profoundly affected by a prolonged campaign of outrages carried out by the I.R.A. between 1956 and 1962, including attacks on public buildings, destruction of public utility installations, and the murders of six policemen.

The type of campaign favoured by militant republicans clearly owed much to the experience of the early 1920s. At that time a large part of Ireland was reduced to a state of conflict, fear and chaos, and from this incoherent situation the republicans had extracted a substantial political success. Subsequently militant republican strategy in Northern Ireland had been given its direction by an instinctive desire to re-create that situation; and such an approach naturally appealed to the spirit of uneasy revolutionary nihilism which had shown itself in many young people in many countries of the world. Anything that created conflict, dislocation, dismay and fear was therefore an acceptable weapon, and the stimulation of a 'backlash' of opposing violence on the other side was also quite an acceptable part of the total strategy.

The outrages of the 1950s and 1960s were endured with great outward calm in Northern Ireland. There was no attempt at reprisals or other adverse reaction. Nevertheless a powerful backlash was built up and the several movements headed by the Reverend Ian Paisley gained much impetus.

At the same time a Protestant terrorist group was established. Illegal and banned, as was the I.R.A., it was also much smaller and poorly organised. It was called the U.V.F., after the old Ulster Volunteer Force which was formed before 1914—a use of an old and honoured name which caused great indignation among some of the surviving members of the older body.

Looking back, therefore, at the twenty years of Lord Brookeborough's government, one can see that the whole atmosphere was hostile to much that hindsight would like to have seen achieved then. Lord Brookeborough himself was a wise and attractive father figure as he presided over the Ulster scene in those years. He was an accurate judge of affairs and knew the limitations imposed on him by public opinion at that time. He had an easy and friendly personality, genial and sceptical, and was one of the most pleasant and amusing conversationalists as well as one of the shrewdest realists that Ulster political life has produced. During his twenty years of premiership his personal qualities gave to a whole era of public life in the province much of its tone and character. Both in office and in retirement his qualities of leadership have made him a respected and very popular figure not only at home but throughout the Commonwealth.

Lord Brookeborough retired in 1963 and was succeeded by Captain Terence O'Neill, formerly Minister of Finance. Captain O'Neill had shown himself an exceptionally hard worker and a very competent departmental minister and he brought to his new office great vitality and an evident spirit of dedication and idealism. He saw in the expanding Ulster economy the best answer to Ulster's problems. He felt that there was much morbid unreality in many of the political and religious attitudes of the past and that the right and only release from them was to concentrate upon those objectives which ought to give satisfaction to all—the development of the province's resources leading to better standards of living, better housing, more economic security, a higher level of employment and a better material environment.

Experts had already been appointed to report on various aspects of the economic and ecological developments of the province. Professor Sir Robert Matthew was commissioned in 1960 to prepare a survey and plan for the Belfast region, and these were published in the final form in 1964. The recommendations extended far beyond the immediate neighbourhood of Belfast, because they envisaged the development or creation of other expanding population centres in other places, including the new city of Craigavon in the Lurgan-Portadown area and the expansion of certain existing towns. On the economic side these recommendations were endorsed by the government's economic consultant, Professor Thomas Wilson, in a report on economic development in Northern Ireland, published in 1965. In that year also a committe under the chairmanship of the late Sir John Lockwood recommended the establishment of a second university at Coleraine.

The Government went ahead at once to implement these various recommendations. Professor Wilson had recommended specific targets for investment, transport, housing and other developments, and these were made part of a general economic plan. A representative Northern Ireland Economic Council was set up in 1964 'to consider and recommend on means of furthering the economic development of Northern Ireland with particular reference to the provision of employment, the promotion of economic growth and improved economic efficiency'. Its establishment coincided with the publication of a Northern Ireland five-year economic plan for the period up to 1970.

An important preliminary to the setting up of the Council was the establishing of better relations between the government and the trade union movement. Most of the trade unions in Northern Ireland had become affiliated to an Irish Congress of Trade Unions based in Dublin and having a Northern Ireland committee. In view of its own relations with the Republic there were obvious political reasons why this was an unacceptable position from the point of view of the Northern Ireland government. But in July 1964 the Congress modified its constitution to give much more autonomy to its Northern Ireland committee, and the government gave recognition to this committee as an acceptable body to be represented on the Economic Council and of course an acceptable body for other purposes as well.

Many new enterprises were begun in those years. Industrial development continued at a steady pace. In Londonderry thirteen new factories were established in a short time. Training facilities were expanded until, proportionately to the population, there were ten times as many places in government training centres as in Britain and a much higher proportionate output of trained industrial workers. The shipbuilding industry acquired the largest dry dock in the United Kingdom. The city of Belfast embarked on huge schemes for redevelopment and rehousing and for the building of an inner ring road to be linked to the motorways which were extending in several directions from the city into the province. A new bridge was built over Belfast's river.

Captain O'Neill set at all times a personal example in trying to break down social barriers between religious groups. But behind those barriers he was well aware of the old political barriers between the governments in Dublin and Belfast. In effect, his hope was that it should be possible to restore the position envisaged in the treaty of 1925 by which the governments were to 'aid one another in a spirit of neighbourly comradeship', concentrating initially on those areas where co-operation between north and south was socially and economically useful and not politically contentious. Already, in spite of Dublin's non-recognition of the Government of Northern Ireland, and even in times of considerable political tension, agreements had been made between departments of the two governments for various convenient operations of sharing and reciprocity in connection with land drainage and railways.

A more cordial spirit of co-operation was now sought at the highest level. In January 1965 Mr. Sean Lemass, Prime Minister of the Republic, came to Stormont for conversations with Captain O'Neill, who in turn paid a visit to Dublin the following month for further conversations with Mr. Lemass. In doing this Captain O'Neill was clearly not acting out of step with the majority feeling in his own party. He was indeed following in the footsteps of Lord Craigavon. The rapprochement between the two governments was significantly given the formal approval of the Grand Orange Lodge. There was also a later exchange of visits with Mr. Jack Lynch, who succeeded Mr.

Lemass. One gain which emerged was an agreement for the sharing of electrical resources.

In November 1965 the O'Neill government held a general election on the basis of the policies it had been pursuing and received a cordial endorsement from the electorate, being returned to power with an increased majority, the highest that the Unionist party had been given for a dozen years.

It was after this that things began to go sour. Possibly the turning point was the fiftieth anniversary celebration of the 1916 Dublin rising. The attitude of the Northern Ireland government was that if anybody wished to celebrate the anniversary in the province, permission to do so within the limits of good order should be given. But the spectacle of the republican flag being carried through Ulster streets revived memories which stirred intense anger, And in Dublin the atmosphere which the celebration evoked made it impossible for the government there, the prisoner of its own traditions, to take any course that would render the O'Neill-Lemass talks other than largely sterile. When they could not be seen as immediately productive of any good effects, the friendly overtures to Dublin began to be denounced by a section of the Ulster public as betrayals, in spite of their entirely uncommitted nature.

Outside the Belfast summer meeting of the General Assembly of the Presbyterian Church extreme Protestant elements staged an aggressive demonstration which caused concern for the personal safety of the Governor of Northern Ireland and resulted in prosecutions.

However, the spirit of progress and reform continued in Northern Ireland, and the government now tried to face the difficult and long deferred project of reorganising the local government system. In 1967 a white paper was issued on the subject.

Local government and, in particular, housing allocation, was a sore point with the province's minority as it was here that religious discrimination against Roman Catholics was felt to emerge. Yet while particular instances of a disturbing character could be clearly demonstrated, they were of a limited nature. Of the ten thousand tenancies which changed hands each year under local authorities, only a tiny proportion gave rise to complaint. In the whole matter of housing, the Cameron commission of inquiry in 1969 recorded complaints about seven out of the 68 local authorities in Northern Ireland.

But it is the outrageous individual case and not the general rule which excites the strongest feeling. Politically the case history which aroused most feeling was that of the city of Londonderry, a predominantly Roman Catholic town in whose corporation Unionists and Protestants held a narrow majority because of the ward system under which elections took place. Londonderry was also the scene of much unemployment and old housing, both the subject of much protest and complaint. Yet Londonderry had also had more done for it in terms of new industries than any other population centre in the province. In 1968 half the jobs created by government effort in Northern Ireland were in or beside Londonderry. New housing was also coming to Londonderry as much as to other places.

With a view to setting right various causes of dissatisfaction, a Northern Ireland Civil Rights Association was founded in 1967. Inevitably its membership and support tended to be predominantly Roman Catholic and Nationalist or Republican, but the Association endeavoured to limit its field of activity to matters not connected with the constitutional status of Northern Ireland and to avoid bringing in political issues of that nature. Yet from its early days the civil rights movement attracted many who were more concerned with those political issues than with what the Association was trying to achieve.

Civil rights demonstrations came to take the form of marches. When one of these marches was directed by the police in Londonderry to alter its planned route in October 1968, the marchers broke through the police cordon and the day ended in rioting.

The general declared objectives of the civil rights movement were not particularly repugnant to the government, but the topic on which the civil rights leaders chose to concentrate seemed an unreal one, for they took as their slogan 'One man one vote'. This referred to the fact that in Northern Ireland, as in a number of other countries, the local government franchise was confined to the adult occupiers of rateable property and their spouses, which meant that only 694,483 voters had local government votes compared with 933,724 who had parliamentary votes. Those who had no local government vote were of no one social, political or religious group. Many had come to believe that, since more local government finance now came from the government than from the rates, the time had come for making the local government franchise universal; but the issue had not that burning quality of one which involved discrimination against some definite body of people.

The use of the emotive slogan 'One man one vote' suggested, and caused many people, both at home and abroad, to believe that there were people in Northern Ireland who had no votes at all, that votes were denied to people on religious grounds, and various other quite untrue notions. On this rather unreal issue great heat built up. Several demonstrations ended in rioting, and at the same time, with growing frequency, the civil rights demonstrations were confronted by aggressive counter demonstrations mounted by 'loyalists'. The occasional display of the flag of the Irish Republic at civil rights demonstrations aroused much anger amongst the Unionist community and, mingled with the anger, there was fear.

There was violence in Londonderry and Dungannon, a dangerous confrontation in Armagh, a vicious attack by Protestant extremists at Burntollet near Londonderry on a civil rights demonstration march from Belfast to Londonderry which had been organised by the People's Democracy, violence in Newry and continuing disturbances in Londonderry.

The United Kingdom government urged the Northern Ireland government to make concessions and remove causes of grievance. This was promptly and even willingly done. In Londonderry a special commission was established for the city's administration and development. But the more extensive the changes and reforms the greater seemed the tendency towards violence.

In a lull early in 1969 a general election was held. The ruling Unionist party was revealed as deeply split over personalities and over the extent to which concessions ought, in the circumstances of the times, to be made to those who demanded reform. Yet the outcome of the election was the greatest Unionist victory in forty years. Less than a quarter of the votes cast in forty-six contested constituencies went to candidates specifically opposed to the Union, and in the remaining six constituencies five Unionists were returned unopposed and one Nationalist.

Violence continued through the spring of 1969. Several organisations were now at work aiming at causing a breakdown in civil government. A spokesman of the People's Democracy, a body participating in civil rights demonstrations and having as its best known leader Miss Bernadette Devlin, wrote in the May–June, 1969, issue of the *New Left Review,* 'We do not want reform in Northern Ireland, we want revolution in Ireland'. The main drive towards violence was, however, republican and involved the I.R.A. and one or two groups which had originated from it. This in turn led to a reaction by Protestant extremists.

The divisions in the Unionist party displayed those psychological drives which cause people almost universally to display far more bitterness against friends and colleagues whose views are very slightly different from their own than they display against those who are their out-and-out opponents. Captain O'Neill resigned on May 1 1969. In a broadcast to the people of the province he said, 'What you and I were trying to do together was right. Morally right, politically right, right for our country and all who seek to live in peace within it . . . But any leader who wants to follow the course of change can only go so far. For change is an unacceptable thing to many people and inevitably one builds up a barrier of resentment which can make further progress impossible. In my judgment and in that of my good friends whom I have consulted, I have reached that moment'. He was succeeded by Major James Chichester-Clark who carried on a substantially similar policy of seeking both to remove any real grievances and to impose order. There were few cabinet changes.

The early summer was not unduly disturbed; but on 12 August grave rioting and violence broke out, first in Londonderry, and then in Belfast on an exceptional scale, and in several Provincial towns. At the time of writing, the events of August 1969 are still being investigated by a special tribunal under Mr. Justice Scarman, and so the assessment of these events, in which several lives were lost and which were deeply traumatic in their effects, is, as we go to press, still *sub judice.*

When the forces of law and order reached the stage of physical exhaustion the Northern Ireland government asked for the help of the army, and the arrival of troops in the disturbed areas created an uneasy calm. Although Northern Ireland had sometimes been accused by its critics of being a police state it was, in fact, found to be under-policed. A big increase in the Royal Ulster Constabulary establishment has since been authorised.

The situation was now the subject of discussions between the Northern Ireland government and the United Kingdom government. Attempts by the government of the Irish Republic to intervene in London and at the United Nations were brushed aside by the British government.

In essence the agreement between the British government and the government of Northern Ireland was that the British government would undertake full military responsibility for the security of Northern Ireland and would give all necessary military help until peace and normality should be fully restored; and, on its side, the Northern Ireland government would institute a most stringent series of checks and reforms to remove every possible ground of grievance, real or imaginary, which might be made a pretext for violent and unconstitutional action.

The programme of changes and legislation included the appointment of a Parliamentary Commissioner to investigate complaints raised through members of the Northern Ireland Parliament and another Commissioner to investigate complaints raised at local government or other levels, the devising and general adoption of an equitable points system for housing allocation by local authorities, franchise changes which removed the few and slight differences that had existed between the voting systems in Northern Ireland and those in Britain, the establishment of a Ministry of Community Relations and an independent Community Relations Commission, the issuing of plans for the long debated re-organisation of local government and for a central housing authority, the civilianisation and enlargement of the police force and the replacement of the Ulster Special Constabulary by an Ulster Defence Regiment of the British Army.

It cannot be said that these developments caused immediate and universal satisfaction, however useful their long-term effects. So far as the minority was concerned, the immediate effect of the changes was bound to be marginal and little felt. And, on the other hand, on the side of the supporters of the Northern Ireland Government, there was indignation at a policy which seemed to give concessions under duress. In the field of security there were deep misgivings at the changed status of the police and the ending of the Ulster Special Constabulary, both of which forces had given warmly appreciated service. These misgivings were intensified by the well intended but sometimes uncertain quality of the security provided by units of the army in the early stages.

In May 1970 the leaders of the Roman Catholic, Presbyterian, Anglican and Methodist Churches in Northern Ireland issued a joint statement emphatically denying that the cause of the disturbances was religion and pointing to the historic, political and social causes of trouble.

As trouble continued, with riots, bomb outrages and incendiarism, the hand of the strategic organiser was increasingly visible in what happened. The perspective was made still more clear in July 1970, when violence again broke out in the Falls Road area in Belfast and a systematic search for arms revealed large quantities of arms and explosives, many thousands of rounds of ammunition and many incendiary devices and grenades.

From the summer of 1970 onwards, the long-familiar pattern of republican terrorism emerged in incendiary attacks on business houses and the murder of soldiers, police and civilians by mines, bombs and sniping.

Summing up the situation, the Prime Minister, Major Chichester-Clark, said: 'I am convinced that the violence was originated by disciplined subversive elements working to overthrow the state.'

The task and role of the army were becoming clearer and at the same time the long-term rightness of the strictly civil role taken by the Northern Ireland Government was receiving a justification.

But to point to a source of violence is not to end or contain it; for violence is deeply counter-productive and keeps recreating itself. Our story ends with a long task lying ahead for the people of Northern Ireland. Mr. Brian Faulkner, who succeeded Major Chichester-Clark in March, 1971, appealed to a wide range of the Province's party political spectrum for co-operation in the task of putting an end to terrorism, restoring peace and confidence, and resuming the more rapid economic and social progress which had been gaining momentum before violence supervened.

Although violence is important and constitutes news, it was remarkably insignificant in most people's daily lives. People continued to go to work, spent holidays at the seaside, enjoyed themselves, played games and went to parties, were born, married and died, and in most areas of the province saw or heard nothing of the violence that they read about in their newspapers. Compared with what had occurred in the early 1920's the disturbances of the late 1960's were much less grave in the casualties caused or in the extent to which they disrupted normal social and economic life.

Thus, though acts of violence have captured the headlines in recent times, the real story of Ulster is one of splendid achievement. In fifty years a backward province has been transformed by the energy and public spirit of its inhabitants. It has expanded enormously in the productivity of its industry and its agriculture, though once it lagged behind. With annual exports worth £670 million and an annual trade turnover of more than £1,396 million, Northern Ireland has moved out of its economic past.

Life in the province has been transformed. It leads the United Kingdom in post-war house building and in provision of new schools and hospitals, in preservation and protection of natural amenities, in mileage of roads, including trunk roads and motorways. It is ahead, too, in individual expectation of life, and in its record of crime detection and successful prosecutions for criminal offences. For all its troubles it has managed at normal times to have proportionately fewer crimes of violence, fewer sexual offences, fewer broken marriages, fewer illegitimate births than